Tiny Miracles of the Sea

Tiny Miracles of the Sea

Exploring Manta Ray Pup Development

Hurmuz Ain

Spectra Enterprise

CONTENTS

INDEX

In the tremendous spread of the world's seas, where daylight moves on a superficial level and the ensemble of marine life reverberations through the profundities, a surprising excursion unfurls — one that dives into the complexities of manta beam little guy improvement. These lofty animals, with their agile developments and confounding presence, epitomize the verse of the sea. Inside the embroidery of their reality lies a story of birth, development, weakness, and the multifaceted dance of endurance that winds through the inclinations of the untamed ocean.

Manta beams, individuals from the Mobulidae family, are worshipped as envoys of the sea's loftiness. With wingspans that can traverse in excess of twenty feet, they explore the watery domains with style and balance. However, past their stunning size and spellbinding appearance lies a domain of minuscule supernatural occurrences — the frequently neglected excursion of manta beam puppies as they explore the difficulties of early life.

This investigation sets out on a journey into the core of the sea, where manta beam little guy improvement is a demonstration of the flexibility and excellence of life underneath the waves. As we set out on this excursion, the sections unfurl like waves, each noteworthy a layer of the enrapturing story carved into the submerged embroidery. A story consolidates logical interest, environmental importance, and a well established appreciation for the fragile equilibrium that supports life in the secretive and remarkable universe of manta beams.

The Riddle of Manta Beams: A Preface to Little guy Improvement

Before we dive into the little supernatural occurrences of manta beam puppy improvement, disentangling the riddle that encompasses these maritime wonders is basic. Manta beams are not simply animals of the ocean; they are appealling creatures that order consideration and flash interest. The family Mobulidae comprises of two unmistakable species — the reef manta beam (Mobula alfredi) and the maritime manta beam (Mobula birostris).

Their expansive, wing-like pectoral balances drive them through the water, making a deception of trip in the unlimited blue. The cephalic blades that undertaking forward from their heads give them a practically ethereal appearance, adding to their charm. As channel feeders, they assume a vital part in keeping up with the equilibrium of marine biological systems, nimbly floating through the water to polish off microscopic fish and little fish.

Notwithstanding their famous status, manta beams face a heap of difficulties. Living space corruption, environmental change, and designated double-dealing undermine their reality, featuring the earnestness of understanding and safeguarding these delicate goliaths. To see the value in the minuscule supernatural occurrences of manta beam little guy improvement, we should initially appreciate the intricacies of their reality — their ways of behaving, relocations, and the secretive domains they navigate in the untamed sea.

Setting out on the Excursion: Understanding Manta Beam Generation

The excursion into manta beam little guy improvement begins with a more profound investigation of their regenerative secrets. Dissimilar to numerous marine species whose conceptive procedures have been legitimate, manta beam generation remained covered in vagueness for a drawn out period. As of late have specialists started to unwind the mysteries of their conceptive science, denoting a huge step in how we might interpret these maritime riddles.

Manta beams display a type of multiplication known as aplacental viviparity, a technique that includes the interior improvement of incipient organisms without a placenta. Female manta beams bring forth live puppies, an interaction that happens at somewhat rare stretches. The complexities of romance, mating conduct, and the incubation time frame all add to the spellbinding adventure of manta beam propagation.

As we set out on this excursion, we strip back the layers of secret encompassing their conceptive lives, acquiring bits of knowledge into the entrancing customs that go before the introduction of manta beam little guys. The profundities of the sea become a phase for an intricate dance — one that unfurls with elegance, accuracy, and a dash of the unexplored world.

Birth in the Blue: A Display of Life Disclosed

The zenith of manta beam little guy improvement is a display of life — an earth shattering situation that comes to pass in the endlessness of the vast ocean. The introduction of manta beam little guys is a demonstration of the strength of life in the maritime domain, where endurance is a fragile dance among sense and transformation.

The subtleties of the birthing system, the development of little manta beam puppies into the world, and their initial collaborations with the sea flows structure a story that epitomizes the delicacy and relentlessness of life. From the perspective of logical request and a profound respect for the marvels of the regular world, we witness the wonder of birth in the blue — an occasion that rises above the limits of species and associates us to the mind boggling snare of life.

As we submerge ourselves in the tale of manta beam little guy improvement, every part unfurls like a tide, uncovering the interconnectedness of life underneath the waves. It is an excursion of revelation, illumination, and a significant appreciation for the little supernatural occurrences that shape the fate of manta beams in the unfathomable hug of the ocean.

Go along with us as we explore the flows of information, revealing the secrets and wonders of manta beam little guy improvement — an excursion that coaxes us to investigate the profundities of understanding and to wonder about the multifaceted dance of life in the extensive performance center of the sea.

1. **Definition and Introduction to Manta Rays**

    In the sky blue breadths of the world's seas, where daylight channels through the glasslike waters and marine life winds around a many-sided embroidery, one animal varieties stands apart as an image of effortlessness, secret, and superbness — the manta beam. With their unquestionable wing-like pectoral balances and ethereal presence, manta beams order consideration and spellbind the minds of sea devotees, analysts, and preservationists the same. This investigation dives into the definition and prologue to manta beams, revealing insight into their science, conduct, natural importance, and the protection challenges they face.

II. Characterizing Manta Beams

Definition: Manta beams have a place with the family Mobulidae, a gathering of enormous beams inside the request Myliobatiformes. These great marine animals are described by their unmistakable morphology, highlighting expansive pectoral balances that look like wings and a smoothed body. Two essential species fall under the umbrella of manta beams: the reef manta beam (Mobula alfredi) and the maritime manta beam (Mobula birostris). The assignment "manta" is gotten from the Spanish word for shroud or mantle, appropriately depicting the far reaching, cover like appearance of their cephalic balances.

Morphology: Manta beams gloat a wingspan that can outperform seven meters (23 feet), making them among the biggest beams in the sea. Their bodies are smoothed dorsoventrally, and the cephalic balances, which stretch out forward from the head, are a characterizing highlight. Not at all like different beams, manta beams miss the mark on tail spine or stinger, adding to their delicate and non-forceful nature.

III. Scientific categorization and Phylogeny

Family Mobulidae: Manta beams are ordered under the family Mobulidae, which additionally incorporates fiend beams. This family is important for the subclass Elasmobranchii, incorporating sharks and beams. Manta beams share normal lineage with different beams however have developed unmistakable qualities that put them aside.

Sort Mobula: Inside the family Mobulidae, manta beams are ordered under the variety Mobula. While the two essential species, reef manta beams (Mobula alfredi) and maritime manta beams (Mobula birostris), share similitudes, they display a few distinctions in conveyance, conduct, and morphology.

IV. The Confounding Idea of Manta Beams

Great Presence: Manta beams are prestigious for their magnificent presence as they nimbly explore the maritime flows. Their cadenced developments, looking like an artful dance in the water, summon a feeling of miracle and reverence. The sheer size and polish of manta beams make them charming diplomats of the marine world.

Channel Feeders: Manta beams are channel feeders, basically consuming microscopic fish and little fish. Their taking care of technique includes swimming with their mouths open, permitting water to go through particular gill rakers while holding prey. This extraordinary strategy for channel taking care of highlights their natural significance in keeping up with the equilibrium of marine environments.

V. Dispersion and Living space

Manta Beam Areas of interest: Manta beams are dispersed across tropical and subtropical waters, leaning toward explicit areas of interest that act as basic environments. Remarkable areas incorporate coral reefs, cleaning stations, and regions with bountiful tiny fish. Perceiving these areas of interest is fundamental for preservation endeavors, as they feature regions where human exercises might influence manta beam populaces.

Worldwide Presence: Manta beams possess a different scope of areas, from the coral-rich waters of the Maldives to the vast sea territories close to Bali. While the reef manta beam will in general continuous shallower waterfront regions, the maritime manta beam is known for its pelagic propensities, frequently wandering into profound waters.

VI. Biological Importance

Cornerstone Species: Manta beams assume a critical part as cornerstone species, impacting the construction and working of marine environments. By controlling populaces of little prey life forms, they add to the wellbeing and equilibrium of the food web. Their presence impacts the overflow and appropriation of microscopic fish, affecting the whole marine local area.

Coral Reef Network: In coral reef environments, manta beams add to supplement cycling and coral wellbeing. Their developments among reefs and cleaning stations improve network, encouraging hereditary variety and flexibility among coral populaces. This biological network highlights the interconnectedness of marine life.

VII. Dangers to Manta Beams

Territory Corruption: Manta beams face huge dangers, with natural surroundings debasement being an essential concern. Beach front turn of events, contamination, and environmental change add to the decay of coral reefs and other basic territories, affecting the accessibility of reasonable conditions for manta beams.

Overfishing: Designated overfishing and bycatch present direct dangers to manta beam populaces. By and large, manta beams were pursued for their gill plates, which are incorrectly accepted to have therapeutic properties. Notwithstanding global security endeavors, unlawful fishing and exchange keep on jeopardizing these marine monsters.

VIII. Protection Status and Endeavors

IUCN Red Rundown: The two types of manta beams are delegated weak on the Global Association for Preservation of Nature (IUCN) Red Rundown. This assignment mirrors the unsettling decrease in their populaces because of different anthropogenic dangers.

Assurance Measures: Perceiving the requirement for preservation, global endeavors have been made to safeguard manta beams. The Show on Worldwide Exchange Imperiled Types of Wild Fauna and Vegetation (Refers to) has recorded manta beams in Addendum II, controlling their global exchange. Moreover, different nations have carried out defensive measures, including the foundation of marine safeguarded regions and guidelines against fishing and hunting.

IX. Human-Manta Beam Communication

The travel industry Effect: The notoriety of manta beam the travel industry has taken off as of late, giving financial advantages to nearby networks and bringing issues to light about manta beam protection.

Nonetheless, unregulated the travel industry can present dangers, including unsettling influence to normal ways of behaving and living space corruption. Executing mindful the travel industry rehearses is pivotal for guaranteeing an amicable conjunction.

Logical Exploration: Researchers and scientists assume a significant part in propelling comprehension we might interpret manta beams. Research projects zeroed in on manta beam conduct, relocation examples, and populace elements contribute important information for protection drives. Cooperative endeavors between researchers, legislatures, and nearby networks improve preservation techniques.

2. Significance of Studying Manta Ray Pup Development

In the far reaching and baffling domains of the world's seas, underneath the undulating surface and inside the mind boggling biological systems of coral reefs and untamed waters, manta beams reveal a dazzling adventure of life. Inside this story, the investigation of manta beam little guy improvement arises as a basic boondocks, offering bits of knowledge into the science, conduct, and natural significance of these maritime monsters. This investigation digs into the significant meaning of exploring manta beam little guy improvement, an excursion that rises above logical interest and reaches out into the domains of protection, environmental equilibrium, and the fragile dance of life underneath the waves.

1. **Understanding the Existence Pattern of Manta Beams**
   1.1. Conceptive Secrets:
   The existence pattern of manta beams, especially the beginning phases including little guy improvement, has extended stayed hidden in secret. Disentangling the complexities of manta beam propagation uncovers an exceptional and intriguing story of romance, mating conduct, and the ensuing incubation time frame. Dissimilar to numerous marine species, manta beams display a type of generation known as aplacental viviparity, where incipient organisms grow inside without a placenta. The investigation of these regenerative cycles gives primary information, permitting researchers to appreciate the variables affecting populace elements and conceptive achievement.

   1.2. Birth and Early Days:
   The birthing system and the underlying phases of a manta beam little guy's life are vital parts of their life cycle. From the second a little guy enters the world to its initial communications with the sea climate, these stages offer windows into the difficulties and weaknesses looked by the youthful beams. Understanding the birth cycle illuminates preservation endeavors, revealing insight into the basic environments and conditions vital for the endurance of manta beam puppies.

2. **Environmental Importance and Biological system Elements**
   2.1. Cornerstone Species Commitment:
   Manta beams, as channel feeders, assume a urgent part in forming marine environments. By controlling the populaces of little prey organic entities, they go about as cornerstone species, affecting the overflow and circulation of tiny fish and other marine life. The investigation of manta beam little guy improvement adds to how we might interpret their biological job, stressing the interconnectedness of marine species and the sensitive equilibrium that supports maritime biodiversity.

   2.2. Coral Reef Availability:
   In coral reef biological systems, manta beams improve availability between reefs through their developments and ways of behaving. The investigation of little guy advancement gives experiences into the manners by which manta beams add to coral wellbeing, hereditary variety, and by and large reef versatility. This understanding illuminates preservation methodologies pointed toward protecting manta beams as well as the more extensive biological systems they possess.

3. **Preservation Suggestions and Danger Alleviation**
   3.1. Danger Appraisal:
   The weaknesses of manta beam puppies during their beginning phases feature

the potential dangers they face from human exercises and natural changes. The investigation of little guy improvement empowers researchers to survey the effect of natural surroundings debasement, environmental change, and overfishing on manta beam populaces. By recognizing and evaluating these dangers, preservationists can plan designated procedures to moderate the dangers and safeguard basic territories.

3.2. Protection Status and The executives:

The preservation status of manta beams is unpredictably attached to their regenerative achievement and little guy endurance. The experiences acquired from concentrating on little guy improvement add to the appraisal of populace wellbeing and elements. Preservation measures, like the foundation of marine safeguarded regions, guidelines against fishing and hunting, and local area based drives, can be educated by a complete comprehension regarding manta beam little guy improvement.

4. **Progressing Logical Information and Exploration**

4.1. Logical Request:

The investigation of manta beam little guy improvement fills in as a foundation for progressing logical information in sea life science and nature. Scientists dig into the intricacies of conceptive life structures, undeveloped turn of events, and early life ways of behaving, adding to the more extensive comprehension of elasmobranch science. This information isn't just imperative for manta beam preservation yet additionally advances our cognizance of the different procedures utilized by marine species for endurance and proliferation.

4.2. Bits of knowledge into Elasmobranch Science:

Elasmobranchs, a subclass of cartilaginous fish that incorporates sharks and beams, display novel regenerative techniques. The investigation of manta beam little guy advancement gives important bits of knowledge into elasmobranch science, with suggestions for the preservation of related species. Relative examinations across elasmobranchs improve how we might interpret developmental variations, conceptive variety, and natural jobs inside marine biological systems.

5. **Instructive and Effort Open doors**

5.1. Rousing Sea Stewardship:

The appealling idea of manta beams, combined with the charming parts of little guy advancement, presents unmatched open doors for schooling and effort. Bringing the miracles of the submerged world to the front draws in crowds, everything being equal, encouraging a feeling of marvel and appreciation for marine life. Instructive projects based on manta beam little guy advancement act as impetuses for sea stewardship, rousing people to become advocates for marine preservation.

5.2. Resident Science Drives:

Connecting with people in general in manta beam research through resident science drives improves information assortment and advances a feeling of local area contribution. With progressions in innovation, people can add to checking manta beam populaces, following developments, and, surprisingly, taking part in distinguishing proof endeavors. Resident science cultivates a cooperative way to deal with marine exploration and preservation, making a worldwide organization of educated and engaged sea devotees.

6. **Future Bearings and Cooperative Exploration**

6.1. Tending to Information Holes:

While critical steps have been made in understanding manta beam little guy advancement, there remain information holes that warrant further investigation. Future examination could zero in on angles like the impact of natural variables on little guy endurance, the job of maternal consideration, and the drawn out ways of behaving of adolescent manta beams. Addressing these holes adds to a more exhaustive comprehension of manta beam life history.

6.2. Cooperative Drives:

The investigation of manta beam little guy advancement benefits from cooperative drives that unite researchers, protection associations, state run administrations, and nearby networks. Cooperative exploration endeavors guarantee a comprehensive way to deal with understanding the intricacies of manta beam life cycles and add to the improvement of viable preservation techniques. By cultivating associations and information trade, mainstream researchers can make progress toward the common objective of safeguarding manta beams and their living spaces.

C. Overview of the Book's Purpose and Structure

As we set out on an enamoring venture into the submerged domains, this book unfurls the pages of a story committed to the little marvels of manta beam little guy improvement. Our motivation is clear — to enlighten the secrets, intricacies, and miracles that include the beginning phases of life for these maritime monsters. Manta beams, with their superb presence and baffling ways of behaving, become heroes in a story that rises above logical request, venturing into the domains of preservation, training, and dazzling appreciation for the fragile dance of life underneath the waves.

1. **The Reason: Disentangling the Privileged insights of Manta Beam Little guy Improvement**

1.1. Logical Investigation:

At the center of this book lies a logical undertaking into the complexities of manta beam little guy improvement. The intention is to unwind the mysteries of their conceptive science, birth processes, and early life stages. By diving into the logical subtleties, we mean to add to the developing assemblage of information encompassing elasmobranch science and, all the more explicitly, the novel attributes that characterize manta beams.

1.2. Protection Basic:

Past logical interest, the reason reaches out to the pressing domain of preservation. Manta beams face various dangers, from natural surroundings corruption to designated fishing, and understanding the weaknesses of their initial life stages is critical for viable protection procedures. The experiences acquired through this investigation expect to illuminate and move preservation endeavors, encouraging a promise to safeguard the territories and conditions indispensable for manta beam little guy endurance.

2. **The Design: Exploring Parts of Disclosure**

2.1. Introduction: The Conundrum of Manta Beams:

The excursion starts with an introduction that sets the stage by unwinding the conundrum of manta beams. This initial section investigates the notorious idea of these maritime goliaths, diving into their morphology, ways of behaving, and environmental importance. It gives the scenery against which the minuscule wonders of manta beam little guy advancement unfurl.

2.2. Part One: The Secrets of Manta Beam Propagation:

The principal section digs into the secrets of manta beam generation, a domain that has long baffled researchers. From romance customs to mating ways of behaving, this part disentangles the complexities that go before the inception of manta beam little guy advancement. It establishes the groundwork for understanding the developmental systems utilized by these marine marvels.

2.3. Section Two: Birth in the Blue: An Exhibition of Life Divulged:

The subsequent section transports perusers into the entrancing exhibition of manta beam birth. It investigates the birthing system, the development of minuscule little guys into the immeasurability of the vast ocean, and their underlying associations with the maritime climate. This part uncovers the sensitive harmony among intuition and variation that characterizes the beginning of manta beam little guys.

2.4. Part Three: Weaknesses and Dangers during Early Life:

The third part moves concentration to the weaknesses and dangers looked by manta beam puppies during their initial life stages. From human-incited dangers to ecological difficulties, this part reveals insight into the dangers that shape the endurance account of these minuscule marine marvels. It accentuates the direness of tending to these dangers for the protection of manta beams.

2.5. Part Four: Maternal Direction and Insurance:

Part four investigates the significant job of maternal direction and security in the advancement of manta beam puppies. From expected maternal procedures to the elements of mother-little guy communications, this section features the multifaceted snare of connections that add to the endurance and prosperity of manta beam puppies.

2.6. Part Five: Development and Advancement:

The fifth part unfurls the excursion of development and advancement in manta beam puppies. From the physiological changes to conduct variations, perusers witness the change of these little creatures into maritime diplomats. This part gives experiences into the elements affecting their development directions.

2.7. Part Six: Taking care of Propensities and Diet of Manta Beam Little guys:

Part six explores the taking care of propensities and dietary inclinations of manta beam puppies. As they change from early life stages to adolescent stages, understanding their dietary requirements and taking care of ways of behaving becomes urgent. This section investigates the dietary complexities that support the development and imperativeness of manta beam little guys.

2.8. Section Seven: Protection Difficulties:

The last part tends to the overall protection challenges looked by manta beam puppies and their grown-up partners. From anthropogenic dangers to the requirement for territory conservation, this part orchestrates the data introduced all through the book into a source of inspiration. It rouses perusers to participate in preservation endeavors and become stewards of the seas.

Chapter 1

Manta Ray Basics

The sea, with its immense and puzzling profundities, has a heap of enrapturing marine animals, among which the manta beam remains as a demonstration of nature's marvels. In this investigation of "Manta Beam Essentials," we leave on an excursion to figure out the life structures, physiology, species variety, territories, and the basic job these magnificent animals play in marine biological systems.

1. **Life systems and Physiology of Manta Beams**

   Manta beams, having a place with the Mobulidae family, are recognized by their enormous, straightened bodies and particular cephalic balances, frequently alluded to as "wings." These wings, traversing up to 25 feet or more, empower manta beams to float smoothly through the water, charming onlookers with their apparently easy developments.

   Underneath their exquisite outside lies a mind boggling life structures streamlined for life in the sea. Manta beams have a cartilaginous skeleton, a trademark imparted to their direct relations, the sharks. This transformation makes them lightweight and lithe, ideal for exploring the tremendous sea breadths.

   One of the most fascinating elements of manta beams is their gill rakers, particular designs that channel microscopic fish and little prey from the water. Dissimilar to many channel taking care of species, manta beams display a one of a kind strategy for taking care of known as "slam filtration." They swim with their mouths completely open, permitting water to disregard their gill rakers and catching tiny creatures for food.

2. **Various Types of Manta Beams**

   Inside the manta beam family, two essential species are perceived: the reef manta beam (Mobula alfredi) and the maritime manta beam (Mobula birostris). While these species share numerous normal qualities, they additionally show qualifications in their appropriation, size, and environmental inclinations.

   The reef manta beam, frequently experienced in waterfront regions and around coral reefs, will in general have a more modest wingspan, normally going from 9 to 15 feet. Conversely, the maritime manta beam, known for its presence in more profound seaward waters, flaunts a bigger wingspan, for certain people arriving at up to 29 feet. Understanding these species differentiations is fundamental for unwinding the more extensive biological embroidered artwork where manta beams exist.

3. **Natural surroundings and Dispersion**

Manta beams are occupants of tropical and subtropical waters, possessing different marine conditions. From waterfront regions to open seas, these animals show a noteworthy versatility to different territories. Seaside natural surroundings, wealthy in tiny fish and other little creatures, draw in the reef manta beams, while the maritime manta beams adventure into more profound waters, following transient examples and maritime flows.

The dissemination of manta beams is a subject of continuous exploration, with researchers utilizing progressed following innovations to reveal relocation courses and better grasp their developments. These glorious animals, with their boundless environments, contribute essentially to the wellbeing and equilibrium of marine biological systems.

4. **Manta Beam Romance and Mating Conduct**

Manta beam romance and mating ways of behaving are many-sided shows that mirror the intricacy of their social connections. Romance frequently includes gymnastic presentations, with male manta beams exhibiting their deftness and ability to draw in expected mates. These submerged ballet productions, portrayed by flips, rolls, and smooth moves, add to the arrangement of mating matches.

When a mating pair shapes, the male purposes particular claspers to move sperm into the female's regenerative lot. Manta beams, in the same way as other different elasmobranchs, display interior treatment, guaranteeing the endurance of the prepared eggs in the difficult marine climate.

5. **Regenerative Cycles and Procedures**

Understanding the regenerative patterns of manta beams reveals the striking techniques these animals utilize to guarantee the endurance of their species. Manta beams show a biennial conceptive cycle, with females ordinarily conceiving an offspring like clockwork. This lengthy span proposes a cautious harmony between conceptive endeavors and the vigorous requests of incubation.

A charming part of manta beam multiplication is the idea of early stage diapause. This peculiarity permits females to defer the implantation of prepared eggs, decisively timing the introduction of their little guys to harmonize with great natural circumstances. The complexities of manta beam conceptive methodologies feature the surprising transformations these animals have developed to flourish in the powerful maritime domain.

6. **Pregnancy and Incubation**

   Manta beam pregnancy is a wonder of nature, described by the development of a solitary little guy inside the mother's belly. The growth time frame changes among species however ordinarily goes on for about a year. During this time, the female focuses profoundly on feeding and safeguarding the creating little guy.

   Maternal consideration assumes a urgent part in manta beam little guy improvement. The mother gives supplements to the developing little guy through a yolk sac placenta, guaranteeing its prosperity until birth. This close association among mother and little guy lays out an establishment for the puppy's initial endurance and improvement in the difficult marine climate.

7. **Birth Interaction of Manta Beam Puppies**

   The birth interaction of manta beam puppies is a pivotal occasion, denoting the perfection of long stretches of development. In contrast to a few different elasmobranchs, for example, sharks, manta beams bring forth live and full fledged little guys. The mother removes the little guy from her body, and the infant manta beam starts its free excursion in the untamed sea.

   The weakness of manta beam little guys during this beginning phase highlights the significance of maternal insurance. The mother stays near her posterity, giving direction, assurance, and amazing open doors for the little guy to acquire fundamental basic instincts. This basic time of maternal consideration shapes the little guy's capacity to explore the difficulties of the marine climate.

8. **Weaknesses and Dangers during Early Life**

   Regardless of the defensive estimates given by maternal consideration, manta beam puppies face various weaknesses during their initial days. Predation from bigger marine species, like sharks and orcas, represents a consistent danger. Moreover, human-prompted difficulties, for example, trap in fishing stuff and contamination, further compound the dangers looked by these youthful marine occupants.

   Understanding the weaknesses of manta beam puppies is significant for creating successful protection techniques. Preservation endeavors should address both normal dangers and human-incited stressors to guarantee the proceeded with endurance of these amazing animals through their developmental stages.

9. **Maternal Direction and Assurance**

   Maternal direction and assurance are instrumental in forming the endurance senses and ways of behaving of manta beam little guys. The mother's presence gives a place of refuge to the little guy to master fundamental abilities, like chasing after food and staying away from expected hunters. The bond laid out among mother and little guy during these early days adds to the general strength of manta beam populaces.

   Perceptions of maternal direction offer important experiences into the social designs and ways of behaving of manta beams. Concentrating on these collaborations improves how we might interpret the many-sided connections inside manta beam populaces, establishing the groundwork for powerful protection systems that focus on the prosperity of both grown-up beams and their weak posterity.

10. **Taking care of Propensities and Diet of Manta Beam Little guys**

The taking care of propensities for manta beam puppies assume a significant part in their development and improvement. While they start with an eating routine of supplement rich milk from their mom, the progress to free taking care of is a basic achievement. Manta beams are channel feeders, and their eating regimen principally comprises of tiny fish and little fish.

The novel construction of their gill rakers permits them to channel tiny creatures from the water proficiently. As manta beam little guys refine their taking care of strategies, they become progressively capable at extricating sustenance from the immense maritime smorgasbord. This variation supports the singular puppies as well as adds to the more extensive biological equilibrium by controlling tiny fish populaces.

11. **Formative Stages: From Little guy to Adolescent**

The formative phases of manta beam little guys reach out past the beginning of weakness, prompting the steady progress from little guy to adolescent. This extraordinary excursion includes the securing of abilities fundamental for free living in the untamed sea. As manta beams develop, their wingspan increments, and their capacity to cover tremendous distances gets to the next level.

The change from little guy to adolescent denotes a time of expanded investigation and collaboration with the marine climate. Manta beams assume vital parts in sea environments, adding to the guideline of prey populaces and keeping up with the equilibrium of marine food networks. Understanding the formative phases of manta beams is critical to valuing their more extensive biological importance.

12. **Associations with the Climate and Other Marine Life**

Manta beams, as cornerstone species, have significant cooperations with their current circumstance and other marine life. Their job as channel feeders impacts the dispersion and wealth of tiny fish, affecting the whole marine food web. Moreover, manta beams take part in harmonious associations with cleaner fish, giving a striking illustration of the interconnectedness of marine environments.

The complex dance of manta beams inside the maritime domain features the sensitive equilibrium that supports marine life. Their associations with different species add to the general strength of coral reefs and beach front environments. Protecting the natural surroundings that help these communications is fundamental for guaranteeing the proceeded with flourishing of manta beams and the environments they possess.

13. **Human Dangers and Preservation Difficulties**

    While manta beams explore the difficulties presented by regular hunters and natural changes, human-incited dangers present huge deterrents to their endurance. Overfishing, driven by the interest for manta beam items, for example, gill plates, represents an extreme danger to worldwide populaces. Environmental change, territory debasement, and plastic contamination further compound the difficulties looked by these maritime goliaths.

    Preservation challenges request a multi-layered approach that joins logical exploration, strategy promotion, and local area commitment. Endeavors to control unlawful fishing, lay out marine safeguarded regions, and advance supportable the travel industry rehearses are basic parts of shielding manta beams and their natural surroundings.

14. **Protection Endeavors and Examples of overcoming adversity**

    In the midst of the overwhelming difficulties, committed protection endeavors and examples of overcoming adversity give good omens to the fate of manta beams. Nations and associations overall are executing measures to safeguard these animals, including the foundation of marine stores and the requirement of fishing guidelines. Cooperative drives between specialists, preservationists, and nearby networks add to a worldwide development pointed toward saving manta beam populaces.

    Examples of overcoming adversity highlight the flexibility of manta beams whenever allowed the opportunity to recuperate. Populace bounce back and positive biological effects exhibit the adequacy of protection drives. These accounts motivate proceeded with endeavors to address the main drivers of manta beam decline and advance supportable practices that benefit both marine life and human networks.

15. **Significance of Protecting Manta Beam Living spaces for Little guy Advancement**

    The conservation of manta beam living spaces is vital for guaranteeing the effective advancement of little guys and the general soundness of manta beam populaces. Seaside regions, favorable places, and transitory courses should be shielded to give basic conditions to mating, growth, and the beginning phases of little guy life.

    Safeguarding these territories goes past the quick advantage to manta beams; it adds to the protection of whole marine biological systems. Solid living spaces support a different cluster of marine life, advancing biodiversity and flexibility notwithstanding natural difficulties. Perceiving the interconnectedness of marine living spaces highlights the significance of all encompassing protection draws near.

16. **Mechanical Advances in Concentrating on Manta Beam Little guy Improvement**

Mechanical advances have reformed the investigation of manta beam little guy improvement, offering specialists extraordinary bits of knowledge into their ways of behaving and developments. Satellite labeling, acoustic telemetry, and submerged drones give significant information on manta beam movement designs, taking care of propensities, and regenerative cycles.

These innovative apparatuses empower researchers to follow individual manta beams over tremendous distances, uncovering beforehand obscure parts of their lives. The reconciliation of state of the art innovation into research endeavors improves our capacity to screen populaces, evaluate protection systems, and adjust the board rehearses to assist manta beams and their living spaces.

17. **Following and Checking Manta Beam Little guys**

The capacity to track and screen manta beam little guys is integral to unwinding the secrets of their initial turn of events. Scientists use satellite and acoustic labels to follow the developments of individual beams, revealing insight into their movement courses, taking care of grounds, and cooperations with other marine species.

Following manta beam little guys gives basic data to preservation endeavors, recognizing key living spaces and relocation halls that require insurance. The information gathered through following drives add to an exhaustive comprehension of manta beam nature, illuminating proof based preservation gauges and guaranteeing the drawn out endurance of these maritime miracles.

18. **Cooperative Drives and Exploration**

Cooperative drives and examination assume an essential part in propelling our insight into manta beam little guy improvement and cultivating compelling protection systems. Global joint efforts unite researchers, traditionalists, policy-makers, and nearby networks to share skill, assets, and experiences.

Research endeavors envelop a large number of disciplines, from sea life science and biology to oceanography and innovation improvement. These cooperative undertakings not just add to the logical comprehension of manta beams yet in addition enable networks to effectively take part in protection drives, making an aggregate obligation to saving these sublime animals and their territories.

19. **Dependable The travel industry and Manta Beam Protection**

The convergence of the travel industry and manta beam protection presents the two difficulties and amazing open doors. Capable the travel industry works on, stressing moral and maintainable communications with manta beams, can add to protection endeavors.

Instruction and mindfulness programs focused on sightseers and neighborhood networks cultivate a feeling of stewardship, empowering rehearses that focus on the prosperity of manta beams and their natural surroundings.

Laying out rules for natural life seeing, advancing capable jumping and swimming practices, and supporting local area based ecotourism drives are vital parts of an all encompassing way to deal with mindful the travel industry. By adjusting financial interests to preservation objectives, dependable the travel industry turns into an incredible asset for safeguarding manta beams and advancing the drawn out manageability of marine conditions.

20. **Offsetting The travel industry with Protection**

Adjusting the developing interest for manta beam the travel industry with preservation objectives requires a sensitive balance. The executives systems that focus on the government assistance of manta beams, for example, carrying out review guidelines, laying out safeguarded regions, and advancing dependable the travel industry rehearses, add to practical concurrence.

Local area association and commitment are fundamental in this equilibrium. Neighborhood people group, frequently reliant upon the travel industry for financial food, assume a urgent part in defending manta beams and their natural surroundings. Cooperative drives that engage networks to effectively take part in preservation endeavors encourage a common obligation regarding safeguarding these marine miracles for people in the future.

1.1 Anatomy and Physiology of Manta Rays

In the immense field of the world's seas, manta beams stand as magnum opuses of development, particularly adjusted to flourish in their amphibian domain. Their life systems and physiology are a demonstration of the style and effectiveness of nature's plan. From their striking size and particular elements to the specific transformations that work with their endurance, the life systems and physiology of manta beams give an enthralling window into the complexities of marine life.

1. **Actual Attributes**

   Manta beams, having a place with the Mobulidae family, are among the biggest beams in the sea. Their leveled bodies are a wonder of hydrodynamics, permitting them to coast easily through the water. One of the most particular elements of manta beams is their cephalic balances, frequently alluded to as "wings" because of their far reaching size. These pectoral balances can traverse up to 25 feet or more, making a dazzling exhibition as they move effortlessly underneath the sea's surface.

   Dissimilar to most hard fish, manta beams have a cartilaginous skeleton, a trademark imparted to their direct relations, the sharks. This cartilaginous design adds to their lightness as well as makes them amazingly deft. The shortfall of a dip bladder, a typical component in hard fish, permits manta beams to change their profundity easily, making them effective and versatile swimmers.

2. **Gill Rakers: Sifting the Sea's Abundance**

   One of the most fascinating parts of manta beam physiology is their taking care of system. Manta beams are channel feeders, depending on specific designs called gill rakers to extricate their food from the water. As they swim with their mouths completely open, water ignores their gill plates, and the gill rakers carry on like a channel, catching tiny fish, little fish, and other infinitesimal organic entities.

Not at all like baleen whales, one more gathering of channel feeders, manta beams utilize a strategy known as "slam filtration." This implies they effectively swim to compel water through their gill rakers, permitting them to target explicit regions wealthy in tiny fish. The productivity of this taking care of technique is fundamental for supporting their energy needs, as they eat huge amounts of food to help their enormous size.

3. **Variations for Effective Swimming**

The body construction of manta beams is finely tuned for productive swimming. Their expansive pectoral balances are a characterizing highlight as well as instrumental in producing lift and moving through the water. These wings are associated with the body major areas of strength for by upholds, permitting manta beams to perform perplexing trapeze artistry and light-footed turns.

The tail, or caudal balance, is moderately little contrasted with the size of their bodies. This smoothed out tail, combined with the undulating movement of their pectoral balances, impels manta beams through the water with effortlessness and accuracy. Their smoothed out shape limits drag, empowering them to cover tremendous distances as they navigate the vast sea.

4. **Extraordinary Tangible Variations**

Manta beams have a variety of tangible transformations that add to their progress in the maritime climate. Their eyes, situated on the sides of their heads, give a wide field of view, permitting them to recognize hunters and expected prey. Regardless of their huge size, manta beams are known for their delicate nature and are many times searched out by jumpers for close experiences.

Notwithstanding vision, manta beams depend on other tangible variations, including electroreception and a specific construction known as the ampullae of Lorenzini. These ampullae are little pores on their heads that distinguish electrical driving forces, helping manta beams explore and find prey in the immensity of the sea.

5. **Conceptive Life structures**

The regenerative life systems of manta beams uncovers captivating experiences into their life cycle. Manta beams display inside treatment, a trademark imparted to different elasmobranchs. Guys have particular regenerative organs called claspers, which are adjusted pelvic balances used to move sperm to the female during mating.

Females have a solitary conceptive lot where preparation happens. The female's capacity to store sperm takes into account controlled generation, with the postponed implantation of prepared eggs adding to the essential timing of little guy births. The regenerative life structures of manta beams is unpredictably connected to their conceptive systems, guaranteeing the endurance of their species in the powerful maritime climate.

6. **The Respiratory Framework**

Like different beams and sharks, manta beams inhale through gills. Their respiratory framework is exceptionally proficient, removing oxygen from the water as it ignores their gill rakers. Dissimilar to a few fish animal varieties that remove oxygen through the two gills and a dip bladder, manta beams depend entirely on their gills for breath.

The gill rakers, beside their job in taking care of, are fundamental for respiratory capabilities. Manta beams are commit smash ventilators, meaning they need to continue to swim to guarantee a nonstop progression of oxygenated water over their gills. This variation stresses the interconnectedness of different physiological cycles in manta beams, adjusting their taking care of and respiratory techniques for ideal endurance.

1.2 Different Species of Manta Rays

Manta beams, among the most charming occupants of the sea, show a noteworthy variety across different species. This variety reaches out past their actual attributes, enveloping contrasts in size, environment inclinations, and natural jobs. In this investigation of various types of manta beams, we dig into the unmistakable attributes that characterize the reef manta beam (Mobula alfredi) and the maritime manta beam (Mobula birostris), revealing insight into the remarkable transformations that add to their endurance in different marine conditions.

1. **Reef Manta Beam (Mobula alfredi)**
   Actual Attributes:
   The reef manta beam, logically known as Mobula alfredi, is described by a marginally more modest size contrasted with its maritime partner. While individual sizes can differ, reef mantas commonly have a wingspan going from 9 to 15 feet. Their straightened bodies and unmistakably formed cephalic blades make them effectively conspicuous submerged.

   Environment and Circulation:
   As the name proposes, reef manta beams are regularly seen as in seaside and reef-rich conditions. They are known to possess tropical and subtropical waters, with an inclination for regions bountiful in microscopic fish and little fish. Well known areas for experiencing reef mantas incorporate coral reefs, tidal ponds, and nearshore waters.

   Conduct and Nature:
   Reef manta beams are frequently connected with explicit cleaning stations, where cleaner fish eliminate parasites and dead skin from their bodies. These cleaning stations assume a vital part in keeping up with the soundness of reef mantas, featuring their environmental interconnectedness with other marine

species. Dissimilar to a few pelagic animal varieties, reef mantas display a more significant level of site constancy, getting back to explicit areas for taking care of, cleaning, and other fundamental exercises.

Preservation Status and Dangers:

While reef manta beams share a few dangers with their maritime partners, for example, entrapment in fishing stuff and living space corruption, they likewise face extraordinary difficulties. Beach front turn of events, contamination, and territory obliteration present critical dangers to their populaces. Preservation endeavors focusing on reef manta beams frequently center around laying out marine safeguarded regions, managing fishing practices, and bringing issues to light about the significance of saving their beach front territories.

2. **Maritime Manta Beam (Mobula birostris)**

Actual Qualities:

The maritime manta beam, logically known as Mobula birostris, holds the title of the world's biggest beam species. With wingspans that can surpass 29 feet, these maritime monsters order consideration as they nimbly explore untamed waters. The maritime manta's bigger size is a key distinctive component from the reef manta, underlining the inconstancy inside the manta beam family.

Environment and Dispersion:

Maritime manta beams are all around adjusted to life in pelagic conditions, frequently crossing profound seaward waters. They are known to occupy both tropical and calm seas, showing a more extensive circulation contrasted with reef mantas. Their transitory examples might cover tremendous distances, following maritime flows and searching out regions wealthy in planktonic food sources.

Conduct and Biology:

Maritime mantas are famous for their sea traversing ventures and are much of the time experienced in regions with solid flows that work with supplement upwelling. These flows draw in tiny fish and other little creatures, framing the premise of the manta beam's eating routine. Dissimilar to reef mantas, maritime mantas might show greater and capricious developments, underscoring their flexibility to the unique states of untamed waters.

Preservation Status and Dangers:

Maritime manta beams face comparable dangers to their reef partners, remembering bycatch for fisheries and natural surroundings corruption. Be that as it may, their more extensive dissemination and frequently subtle nature present difficulties for protection endeavors. Worldwide joint effort is pivotal for tending to dangers that range different wards. Endeavors to safeguard maritime mantas frequently include executing fishing guidelines, advancing manageable practices, and utilizing innovation to follow their developments and movements.

3. **Communications Between Species**

While reef and maritime manta beams are unmistakable species, their communications and environmental jobs add to the many-sided equilibrium of marine biological systems. The two species are channel feeders, depending on tiny fish and little living beings for food. In regions where their reaches cross-over, they might share cleaning stations, featuring a level of environmental cross-over.

Regardless of these similitudes, the distinctions in their favored natural surroundings and ways of behaving propose some degree of biological specialty division. Reef mantas, with their fondness for beach front and reef conditions, may assume a vital part in molding the strength of coral biological systems. Conversely, maritime mantas add to the supplement cycling of untamed waters, impacting the appropriation and overflow of planktonic organic entities.

Understanding the elements between various types of manta beams is fundamental for comprehensive protection procedures. Safeguarding their different environments, whether beach front or pelagic, guarantees the proceeded with presence of these remarkable animals and adds to the general soundness of marine biological systems.

4. **Protection Suggestions and Worldwide Drives**

Preserving various types of manta beams requires an extensive methodology that addresses both shared and species-explicit dangers. Worldwide drives, for example, the Show on Global Exchange Jeopardized Types of Wild Fauna and Verdure (Refers to), assume a fundamental part in managing the global exchange of manta beam items. Also, associations like the Manta Trust and Undertaking Manta direct exploration, bring issues to light, and team up with nearby networks to execute preservation measures.

Saving the living spaces pivotal for the endurance of manta beams is fundamental to these preservation endeavors. Laying out marine safeguarded regions, controlling fishing rehearses, and advancing dependable the travel industry are key procedures to guarantee the very much was of these brilliant animals.

1.3 Habitats and Distribution

Manta beams, with their elegant wings and unmistakable presence, are inhabitants of the world's seas, adjusting to a different scope of territories. Their appropriation traverses tropical and subtropical waters, and their decision of natural surroundings differs between species.

Reef manta beams (Mobula alfredi) dominatingly possess beach front regions, coral reefs, and tidal ponds. These nearshore conditions, wealthy in microscopic fish and little fish, give ideal circumstances to taking care of and cleaning conduct. Reef mantas grandstand a level of site devotion, getting back to explicit areas for exercises like mating and taking care of, framing fundamental associations with nearby biological systems.

Then again, maritime manta beams (Mobula birostris) adventure into more profound seaward waters. Their extensive wingspans, arriving at more than 29 feet, prepare them for the powerful states of pelagic conditions. Maritime mantas are known for their transitory examples, following maritime flows that lead to supplement rich regions, supporting their planktonic eating routine. These great voyagers cover immense distances, mirroring their flexibility to the open territories of the world's seas.

The worldwide appropriation of manta beams, formed by the accessibility of food sources and natural circumstances, highlights their importance in keeping up with the equilibrium of marine biological systems. Their living spaces, whether beach front or pelagic, act as significant centers for taking care of, propagation, and other fundamental life exercises.

Saving manta beam environments is indispensable to guaranteeing the endurance of these marine monsters. Dangers like territory corruption, overfishing, and environmental change require coordinated endeavors to lay out marine safeguarded regions, direct fishing rehearses, and advance supportable the travel industry. By understanding the environments and appropriation examples of manta beams, we can figure out compelling protection methodologies that shield these phenomenal animals and the biological systems they call home.

Chapter 2

Mating And Reproduction

Manta beams, with their entrancing effortlessness and puzzling presence in the sea, participate in a dazzling dance of romance, mating, and proliferation. The complexities of their conceptive ways of behaving uncover an intriguing interaction of senses, social elements, and methods for surviving. In this investigation, we dig into the universe of mating and propagation in manta beams, revealing insight into the romance customs, conceptive cycles, and the momentous methodologies that add to the continuation of their species.

1. **Manta Beam Romance: Expressive dance in the Sea**
   The romance ceremonies of manta beams are a movement of style, where male beams grandstand their nimbleness and ability to draw in possible mates. Regularly saw in shallow waters, these romance showcases Include aerobatic moves, flips, rolls, and elegant developments. The ease of their developments, highlighted by their sweeping wings, makes a visual exhibition that enthralls spectators.
   Romance ways of behaving fill different needs. They permit male manta beams to exhibit their wellness and hereditary prevalence over expected mates. The gymnastics may likewise assume a part in invigorating the female's conceptive status. These romance ceremonies are a demonstration of the intricacy of social cooperations inside manta beam populaces.

2. **Mating Conduct: Artful dance Changes to Closeness**
   When romance has effectively unfurled, the mating conduct of manta beams becomes the dominant focal point. The male, furnished with particular conceptive organs called claspers, delicately moves toward the female. The claspers, changed pelvic blades, are utilized to move sperm into the female's regenerative plot.
   Manta beams display inside preparation, an element imparted to different elasmobranchs, guaranteeing the endurance of their posterity in the difficult marine climate. The closeness of the mating ceremonial highlights the association

among male and female beams, making way for the continuation of the manta beam life cycle.

3. **Conceptive Cycles: Biennial Rhythms of Life**

   Manta beams follow a biennial conceptive cycle, with females ordinarily conceiving an offspring like clockwork. This lengthy span between conceptive occasions is a critical part of their regenerative procedure, permitting females to concentrate profoundly on supporting their creating posterity.

   The biennial cadence lines up with the normal elements of their maritime climate. It guarantees that the planning of births compares with positive circumstances, upgrading the possibilities of endurance for manta beam puppies. The synchronization of conceptive cycles among manta beam populaces is a demonstration of the transformative variation that adjusts the vigorous requests of development with the vulnerabilities of the marine climate.

4. **Pregnancy and Incubation: An Excursion Inside**

   After effective mating, female manta beams go through pregnancy and incubation, conveying their creating little guys inside their bodies. The growth time frame fluctuates among species, however it normally goes on for about a year. The inward climate of the mother's belly gives assurance and sustenance to the creating little guy.

   During development, manta beams utilize a remarkable conceptive procedure known as undeveloped diapause. This captivating peculiarity permits females to defer the implantation of prepared eggs, really stopping the advancement of incipient organisms. This essential deferral guarantees that the introduction of manta beam little guys lines up with ideal natural circumstances, improving the probability of their endurance.

   The physiological variations during growth feature the multifaceted associations among mother and little guy. The mother gives supplements to the creating little guy through a yolk sac placenta, guaranteeing its prosperity until birth. This personal association lays out an establishment for the little guy's initial endurance and improvement in the difficult marine climate.

5. **Birth Interaction of Manta Beam Little guys: A Pivotal Occasion**

   The birth interaction of manta beam little guys is a pivotal occasion, denoting the summit of long periods of development. In contrast to a few different elasmobranchs, for example, sharks, manta beams bring forth live and full fledged puppies. The mother removes the little guy from her body, and the infant manta beam starts its free excursion in the untamed sea.

   The weakness of manta beam puppies during this beginning phase highlights the significance of maternal security. The mother stays near her posterity, giving direction, insurance, and open doors for the little guy to master fundamental abilities to survive. This basic time of maternal consideration shapes the little guy's capacity to explore the difficulties of the marine climate.

6. **Weaknesses and Dangers during Early Life: Exploring the Maritime Domain**
Regardless of the security given by maternal consideration, manta beam little guys face various weaknesses during their initial days. Predation from bigger marine species, like sharks and orcas, represents a steady danger.

Moreover, human-prompted difficulties, for example, entrapment in fishing stuff and contamination, further compound the dangers looked by these youthful marine occupants.

The sensitive harmony between regular dangers and human-actuated stressors features the difficulties of early life for manta beam little guys. Protection endeavors should address the two perspectives to guarantee the endurance of these unprecedented animals. Observing and moderating human effects, alongside safeguarding basic environments, assume fundamental parts in getting a future for manta beam populaces.

7. **Maternal Direction and Insurance: Sustaining the Future**
Maternal direction and assurance are instrumental in molding the endurance senses and ways of behaving of manta beam little guys. The mother's presence gives a place of refuge to the little guy to master fundamental abilities, including searching, keeping away from hunters, and exploring the immensity of the untamed sea.

The connection among mother and little guy reaches out past the prompt post-birth time frame. Manta beam moms are known to display proceeded with care and cautiousness, establishing a steady climate for the little guy's development and improvement. This drawn out time of maternal direction adds to the versatility of manta beam populaces, guaranteeing that every age is prepared to confront the difficulties of their maritime domain.

8. **Social Elements and Mutual Ways of behaving: Strength in Numbers**
Manta beams, known for their lone and smooth developments, likewise show mutual ways of behaving, particularly during romance and mating seasons. Conglomerations of manta beams, frequently alluded to as "manta trains" or "manta typhoons," exhibit the social elements inside their populaces.

These get-togethers fill numerous needs, including romance showcases, mating open doors, and cooperations with cleaner fish. The shared ways of behaving of manta beams accentuate the interconnectedness of their lives and feature the significance of social cooperations in their conceptive systems.

9. **Preservation Difficulties: Human-Actuated Dangers**
While the mating, generation, and sustaining ways of behaving of manta beams add to the strength of their populaces, human-actuated dangers present critical difficulties. Overfishing, driven by the interest for manta beam items, for example, gill plates, represents an extreme danger to worldwide populaces. Environmental change, territory debasement, and plastic contamination further compound the difficulties looked by these maritime monsters.

Preservation challenges request a complex methodology that consolidates logical examination, strategy support, and local area commitment. Endeavors to check unlawful fishing, lay out marine safeguarded regions, and advance feasible the travel industry rehearses are basic parts of protecting manta beams and their natural surroundings.

10. **Protection Endeavors and Examples of overcoming adversity: A Hint of something to look forward to**

In the midst of the overwhelming difficulties, devoted preservation endeavors and examples of overcoming adversity give hints of something to look forward to the fate of manta beams. Nations and associations overall are carrying out measures to safeguard these animals, including the foundation of marine stores and the implementation of fishing guidelines. Cooperative drives between scientists, preservationists, and nearby networks add to a worldwide development pointed toward protecting manta beam populaces.

Examples of overcoming adversity highlight the versatility of manta beams whenever allowed the opportunity to recuperate. Populace bounce back and positive natural effects show the adequacy of preservation drives. These accounts move proceeded with endeavors to address the underlying drivers of manta beam decline and advance maintainable practices that benefit both marine life and human networks.

2.1 Manta Ray Courtship and Mating Behavior

Manta beams, with their grand wings and effortless developments, participate in an enamoring dance of romance and mating that mirrors the perplexing social elements and methods for surviving inside their maritime domain. From gymnastic romance presentations to the nuanced ceremonies of mating, the romance and mating conduct of manta beams is an interesting excursion into the profundities of their submerged world. In this investigation, we dig into the complexities of manta beam romance and mating conduct, revealing insight into the novel procedures that guarantee the continuation of their species.

1. **Romance Shows: A Movement of Polish**

   Manta beam romance starts with intricate showcases of class and spryness. Normally saw in shallow waters, male manta beams take part in aerobatic developments that grandstand their solidarity, adaptability, and ability. These showcases include somersaults, rolls, and circles, making an entrancing artful dance in the sea profundities.

   The sweeping wings of manta beams assume a focal part in these romance showcases. The musical undulation of their pectoral blades complements the smoothness of their developments, making a visual scene that draws in possible mates as well as fills in as a show of the male's wellness and hereditary predominance.

   Romance showcases are tied in with drawing in females as well as about laying out strength and order among male manta beams. The opposition for mates is wild, and the most dexterous and talented guys frequently gain the consideration of responsive females. These submerged ballet performances unfurl in the complicated embroidery of coral reefs and seaside regions, where the movement of romance assumes a significant part in the regenerative progress of manta beam populaces.

2. **Social Elements: Get-together in Manta Trains**

   While manta beams are frequently connected with singular and effortless developments, romance and mating seasons achieve an adjustment of their social elements. Conglomerations of manta beams, known as "manta trains" or "manta twisters," feature the collective ways of behaving inside their populaces. These social occasions are not just a demonstration of the interconnectedness of their lives yet in addition fill explicit regenerative needs.

   Manta prepares frequently comprise of various guys competing for the focus of a responsive female. The elements inside these totals include a fragile harmony between contest and participation. The guys show their romance ways of behaving in nearness to the female, making an outwardly striking exhibition of submerged polish.

   Inside these get-togethers, there is proof of social orders and associations among individual manta beams. Prevailing guys might affirm their presence through more articulated romance presentations, while subordinate guys might embrace elective techniques to draw in with females. The social elements inside manta trains give experiences into the intricacy of their regenerative methodologies and the helpful components associated with the romance interaction.

3. **Female Decision and Particular Mating: Evaluating Wellness and Hereditary qualities**

   Female manta beams assume a functioning part in the romance cycle by evaluating the wellness and hereditary nature of likely mates. The aerobatic presentations of male manta beams act as obvious signals that permit females to assess the deftness, strength, and in general wellbeing of the showing people. The decision of a mate is a basic choice for female manta beams, as it impacts the hereditary variety and wellness of their posterity.

   Research recommends that female manta beams might favor guys that show more intricate and vigorous romance presentations. These showcases are characteristic of the male's state of being and conceptive wellness. By choosing mates in view of these showcases, females add to the support of hereditary variety inside the populace and improve the general versatility of manta beam populaces to changing natural circumstances.

   The course of female decision in manta beam romance is a powerful transaction of obvious signals, ecological elements, and the regenerative objectives of the two guys and females. Understanding the systems of female decision gives significant bits of knowledge into the transformative methodologies that have molded the romance and mating ways of behaving of these maritime goliaths.

4. **Mating Conduct: A Delicate Artful dance of Association**

   When romance presentations stand out of an open female, the mating conduct of manta beams becomes the dominant focal point. Mating includes the sensitive association between the male and female, finishing in the exchange of sperm from the male to the female's conceptive parcel.

   Male manta beams are furnished with particular regenerative organs called claspers, which are changed pelvic blades. These claspers assume an essential part in the mating system. The male methodologies the female delicately, adjusting his body to hers to work with the addition of his claspers into the cloaca of the female. The exchange of sperm happens during this cozy second, denoting the zenith of the romance custom.

   Manta beams display inward treatment, a conceptive methodology imparted to different elasmobranchs, like sharks. The inner treatment guarantees that the female's eggs are prepared inside her regenerative lot, expanding the possibilities of effective proliferation in the difficult marine climate. The mating conduct of manta beams mirrors a sensitive expressive dance of association, where actual vicinity and exact developments add to the continuation of their species.

5. **Post-Mating Period: Exploring the Difficulties**

   After fruitful mating, female manta beams go through a post-mating period during which the treated eggs foster inside their bodies. The growth time frame differs among species yet by and large goes on for about a year. Manta beams display an extraordinary conceptive system known as early stage diapause, permitting females to defer the implantation of treated eggs until ideal ecological circumstances are met.

   During this post-mating period, female manta beams explore the difficulties of the marine climate while supporting the creating undeveloped organisms inside their bodies. The physiological variations during incubation, including the arrangement of a yolk sac placenta, guarantee the prosperity of the creating little guys.

   The post-mating time frame is a basic stage in the conceptive excursion of manta beams, and the difficulties looked during this period underscore the strength and flexibility of these marine goliaths. Protection endeavors that address the dangers looked by pregnant females, like natural surroundings corruption and human-instigated stressors, add to the fruitful finishing of the regenerative cycle.

6. **Birth Cycle: A Zenith of Life's Excursion**

   The birth cycle of manta beam puppies is a zenith of the conceptive excursion, denoting the start of another age in the maritime domain. In contrast to a few different elasmobranchs, for example, sharks, manta beams bring forth live and full fledged little guys. The mother ousts the little guy from her body, and the infant manta beam leaves on its free excursion in the vast sea.

The birth cycle is a pivotal occasion, and the weakness of manta beam little guys during their initial days highlights the significance of maternal insurance. The mother stays near her posterity, giving direction, assurance, and open doors for the little guy to master fundamental abilities to survive.

The birth interaction additionally implies the continuation of the manta beam life cycle and the death of hereditary data to the future. The fragile harmony between normal dangers and human-actuated stressors during this beginning phase underlines the requirement for extensive preservation methodologies that safeguard basic environments and guarantee the prosperity of manta beam populaces.

7. **Maternal Consideration and Broadened Direction: Sustaining the Future**
Maternal consideration is a significant part of the manta beam conceptive excursion, reaching out past the quick post-birth time frame. Manta beam moms are known to display proceeded with care and watchfulness, establishing a steady climate for the little guy's development and improvement.

The drawn out time of maternal direction adds to the flexibility of manta beam populaces. Moms give chances to puppies to acquire fundamental abilities, including scrounging, keeping away from hunters, and exploring the immeasurability of the vast sea. This supporting stage lays out an establishment for the little guy's capacity to flourish in the difficult marine climate.

The connection among mother and little guy features the interconnectedness of family structures inside manta beam populaces. Understanding the elements of maternal consideration gives experiences into the social ways of behaving and step by step processes for surviving that add to the progress of these maritime goliaths.

8. **Protection Difficulties and Procedures: Shielding the Artful dance of Life**

While the romance and mating ways of behaving of manta beams are wonders of nature, they face critical preservation challenges that compromise their reality. Overfishing, driven by the interest for manta beam items, natural surroundings debasement, and environmental change present extreme dangers to worldwide manta beam populaces.

Preservation techniques should address both the immediate dangers to manta beams and the more extensive difficulties confronting marine environments. Laying out marine safeguarded regions, controlling fishing rehearses, and advancing manageable the travel industry are fundamental parts of protection endeavors. Furthermore, tending to the underlying drivers of natural surroundings debasement and environmental change is essential for guaranteeing the drawn out endurance of manta beam populaces.

Worldwide drives, for example, the Show on Global Exchange Jeopardized Types of Wild Fauna and Verdure (Refers to), assume an imperative part in directing the worldwide exchange of manta beam items. Cooperative endeavors between specialists, preservation associations, and nearby networks add to a far reaching way to deal with manta beam protection.

2.2 Reproductive Cycles and Strategies

The regenerative cycles and systems of manta beams are a demonstration of the mind boggling equilibrium of timing, transformation, and endurance inside their maritime domain. From the biennial rhythms of multiplication to the essential postponement of early stage improvement, manta beams have developed novel procedures to explore the difficulties of the marine climate. In this investigation, we dive into the entrancing universe of manta beam regenerative cycles and techniques, revealing insight into the transformations that guarantee the continuation of their species.

1. **Biennial Regenerative Cycles: Nature's Synchronized Cadence**

   Manta beams follow a biennial regenerative cycle, an example profoundly imbued in their developmental history. This repeating musicality includes females conceiving an offspring roughly like clockwork. This drawn out stretch between regenerative occasions fills numerous needs, lining up with the normal elements of their maritime climate.

   The biennial regenerative cycle is an essential variation to the difficulties of the marine climate. It permits females to concentrate on supporting their creating posterity while enhancing the planning of births. The synchronization of regenerative cycles among manta beam populaces accentuates the transformative benefit of this system, guaranteeing that the planning of births relates with great natural circumstances.

   This synchronized musicality isn't just an impression of the manta beam's transformation to their current circumstance yet additionally a reaction to the dynamic and capricious nature of the sea. By scattering regenerative occasions, manta beams improve the probability of effective little guy endurance in this present reality where natural circumstances, food accessibility, and different variables can fluctuate broadly.

2. **Early stage Diapause: Vital Deferral for Ideal Circumstances**

   One of the most captivating parts of manta beam conceptive systems is the peculiarity known as early stage diapause. This regenerative variation permits females to defer the implantation of treated eggs until ideal ecological circumstances are met. This essential postponement guarantees that the planning of births lines up with times of overflow and positive conditions for the endurance of manta beam little guys.

   During undeveloped diapause, the advancement of prepared eggs is briefly ended. This respite in undeveloped development empowers females to painstakingly time the introduction of their posterity in view of elements like food accessibility, water temperature, and other ecological factors. The capacity to decisively postpone the advancement of undeveloped organisms mirrors the nuanced variation of manta beams to the always changing states of the sea.

The course of early stage diapause is a complex regenerative procedure that lines up with the manta beam's biennial conceptive cycle. By synchronizing the planning of incubation and birth with ideal ecological circumstances, manta beams increment the possibilities of little guy endurance during those basic beginning phases of life.

3. **Growth Period: Supporting Life Inside**

Whenever mating has happened and prepared eggs have been embedded, female manta beams go through a growth period during which they convey and sustain their creating little guys inside their bodies. The incubation time frame fluctuates among manta beam species however by and large goes on for about a year. This time of inner incubation gives a safeguarded climate to the creating incipient organisms.

The physiological transformations during incubation are amazing. Females structure a yolk sac placenta, a particular design that works with the trading of supplements between the mother and the creating little guy. This supporting association guarantees the prosperity of the little guy and highlights the close connection among mother and posterity.

The growth time frame is a basic stage in the conceptive excursion of manta beams. It includes the cautious designation of assets, energy, and physiological cycles to help the improvement of the future. The progress of incubation adds to the versatility of manta beam populaces and shapes the fate of their maritime heritage.

4. **Birth and Early Life: Exploring the Maritime Domain**

The birth cycle of manta beam puppies is an earth shattering occasion, denoting the finish of development and the start of free life in the untamed sea. Manta beams bring forth live and full grown little guys, a trademark that separates them from a few different elasmobranchs, like sharks.

The weakness of manta beam little guys during their initial days highlights the significance of maternal assurance and direction. Notwithstanding being conceived full fledged, these youthful marine occupants face various difficulties, including predation from bigger marine species and human-actuated dangers like snare in fishing gear.

The early existence of manta beam puppies is a time of fast transformation and learning. Moms give fundamental direction, establishing a steady climate for the improvement of critical basic instincts. The supporting and defensive impulses of manta beam moms add to the strength of their posterity during these developmental stages.

5. **Maternal Consideration: A Delayed Responsibility**

Maternal consideration stretches out past the quick post-birth time frame in manta beams, addressing a delayed obligation to the prosperity of their posterity. Manta beam moms are known to show proceeded with care and watchfulness, guaranteeing that their little guys have the most ideal beginning in the difficult marine climate.

The lengthy time of maternal consideration includes continuous direction, insurance, and amazing open doors for little guys to master fundamental abilities. This responsibility adds to the versatility and flexibility of manta beam populaces, underlining the significance of family structures inside their maritime domain.

The connection among mother and little guy, produced through the phases of development, birth, and early life, is an essential component in the regenerative progress of manta beams. Maternal consideration assumes an essential part in forming the endurance senses and ways of behaving of the future, encouraging an association that adds to the drawn out maintainability of manta beam populaces.

6. **Preservation Suggestions: Safeguarding Regenerative Systems**

Understanding the regenerative cycles and systems of manta beams has critical ramifications for their protection. The biennial conceptive cycle, early stage diapause, and expanded maternal consideration all feature the many-sided variations that manta beams have created to guarantee the endurance of their species.

Preservation endeavors should perceive the weaknesses and difficulties looked by manta beams all through their conceptive excursion. Human-incited dangers, for example, overfishing, environment corruption, and environmental change, present serious dangers to manta beam populaces. Safeguarding basic territories, directing fishing rehearses, and resolving more extensive natural issues are fundamental parts of protection procedures pointed toward shielding the regenerative progress of manta beams.

Moreover, mindfulness and schooling assume critical parts in cultivating a more profound comprehension of the significance of manta beam regenerative cycles.

By advancing mindful the travel industry works on, supporting exploration drives, and upholding for the insurance of these heavenly animals, we can add to the preservation of their interesting regenerative techniques.

2.3 Pregnancy and Gestation

The excursion of manta beam proliferation arrives at an essential stage with pregnancy and growth, where the maritime expressive dance of romance and mating develops into the close sustaining of life inside the immense territory of the vast ocean. The physiological wonder of growth in manta beams includes a progression of variations and techniques that underline the flexibility of these marine monsters. In this investigation, we dive into the unpredictable cycles of pregnancy and growth, revealing insight into the special viewpoints that characterize this vital stage in the existence pattern of manta beams.

1. **Interior Preparation: An Establishment for Growth**

   The regenerative excursion of manta beams starts with interior treatment, an interaction that recognizes them from numerous other marine species. Inward preparation guarantees that the treated eggs are safeguarded inside the female's body, making way for the ensuing phases of pregnancy and growth.

   During mating, male manta beams utilize particular regenerative organs called claspers to move sperm into the female's conceptive plot. This inside preparation is a key variation that improves the possibilities of effective proliferation in the difficult marine climate. The exchange of sperm denotes the inception of the growth cycle, where the female's body goes through wonderful changes to help the advancement of the developing undeveloped organisms.

2. **Incubation Period: An Ensemble of Variations**

   The growth time frame in manta beams is a complicated orchestra of physiological transformations that guarantee the prosperity of the creating puppies. While the particular term of development can differ among manta beam species, it by and large goes on for about a year.

   During this period, the female's body goes through tremendous changes to oblige the creating incipient organisms. One of the striking variations is the development of a yolk sac placenta, a specific construction that works with the trading of supplements between the mother and the developing puppies. This physiological association is fundamental for the sustenance and improvement of the undeveloped organisms inside the defensive climate of the mother's body.

   The development time frame addresses a basic stage in the conceptive excursion of manta beams. As the incipient organisms create, the female's body gives a stable and sustaining climate that guarantees the prosperity of the little guys. The intricate interaction of natural cycles features the complexity of manta beam conceptive methodologies, where incubation fills in as a defend for the future.

3. **Undeveloped Diapause: An Essential Respite Being developed**

   A captivating part of manta beam growth is the peculiarity known as early stage diapause. This conceptive procedure permits females to decisively defer the advancement of treated eggs until ideal ecological circumstances are met. The capacity to stop early stage improvement is a nuanced transformation that adds to the general outcome of manta beam multiplication.

   Undeveloped diapause includes an impermanent suspension of the improvement of prepared eggs, guaranteeing that the planning of birth lines up with good conditions. This essential postponement permits females to synchronize the introduction of their puppies with times of overflow, guaranteeing better possibilities of endurance during the basic beginning phases of life.

The execution of undeveloped diapause mirrors the developmental versatility of manta beams in adjusting to the dynamic and capricious nature of the marine climate. This essential delay being developed features the interconnectedness of regenerative procedures and natural prompts, stressing the fragile equilibrium that supports manta beam populaces.

4. **Supporting the Future: Maternal Consideration and Insurance**

As the growth time frame advances, the mother assumes a significant part in sustaining and safeguarding the creating puppies inside her body. Maternal consideration reaches out past the physiological perspectives and includes a social obligation to the prosperity of the future.

The mother's body gives a solid climate to the developing undeveloped organisms, guaranteeing that they get the fundamental supplements for ideal turn of events. This private association among mother and posterity is a demonstration of the maternal senses and defensive ways of behaving that add to the progress of manta beam multiplication.

The sustaining job of the mother go on past growth, stretching out into the beginning phases of the little guy's life after birth. Manta beam moms are known to display proceeded with care and watchfulness, establishing a strong climate for their posterity to master fundamental abilities. This lengthy time of maternal direction adds to the flexibility and versatility of manta beam populaces, supporting the significance of family structures inside their maritime domain.

5. **Preservation Contemplations: Safeguarding Incubation Shelters**

Understanding the complexities of pregnancy and growth in manta beams is fundamental for viable preservation endeavors. The growth time frame addresses a weak stage in the conceptive excursion, where outside dangers like territory corruption, contamination, and human-prompted stressors can affect the prosperity of pregnant females and creating little guys.

Moderating incubation territories is a basic part of manta beam insurance. Laying out marine safeguarded regions that incorporate key development locales guarantees that these regions stay undisturbed and give a place of refuge to pregnant females. Furthermore, tending to more extensive protection challenges, for example, overfishing and environmental change, adds to the safeguarding of the circumstances fundamental for fruitful incubation and propagation.

Chapter 3

Birth And Early Days

The birth and beginning of manta beams mark a basic stage in their life cycle, addressing a progress from the safeguarded climate of development to the difficulties of free life in the vast sea. This period includes the climax of the growth interaction, the special qualities of manta beam births, and the weaknesses and transformations of little guys during their initial days.

1. **Birth Interaction: A Pivotal Occasion**

   Manta beams, not at all like a few different elasmobranchs, bring forth live and full fledged little guys. The birth cycle is an earth shattering occasion, commonly happening in unambiguous areas that offer a level of security for both mother and posterity. The mother removes the little guy from her body, and the infant manta beam starts its autonomous excursion in the immensity of the vast sea.

   The attributes of manta beam births, including the size and number of puppies, may change among species. Understanding the subtleties of the birth cycle gives experiences into the conceptive methodologies and variations that add to the endurance of manta beam populaces.

2. **Weaknesses and Dangers during Early Life**

   Regardless of the assurance given by maternal consideration, manta beam puppies face various weaknesses during their initial days. Predation from bigger marine species, like sharks and orcas, represents a steady danger. Also, human-prompted difficulties, remembering entrapment for fishing stuff and contamination, further compound the dangers looked by these youthful marine occupants.

   The sensitive harmony between regular dangers and human-incited stressors highlights the difficulties of early life for manta beam puppies. Preservation endeavors should address the two viewpoints to guarantee the endurance of these unprecedented animals. Observing and relieving human effects, alongside safeguarding basic natural surroundings, assume fundamental parts in getting a future for manta beam populaces.

3. **Maternal Direction and Assurance**

   Maternal direction and security are instrumental in molding the endurance impulses and ways of behaving of manta beam puppies. The mother's presence gives a place of refuge to the little guy to master fundamental abilities, including searching, staying away from hunters, and exploring the immensity of the untamed sea.

   The connection among mother and little guy reaches out past the quick post-birth time frame. Manta beam moms are known to display proceeded with care and cautiousness, establishing a steady climate for the little guy's development and improvement. This lengthy time of maternal direction adds to the strength of manta beam populaces, guaranteeing that every age is prepared to confront the difficulties of their maritime domain.

4. **Social Elements and Public Ways of behaving**

   Manta beams, known for their single and agile developments, additionally display public ways of behaving, particularly during the beginning of puppies. Collections of manta beams, frequently alluded to as "manta trains" or "manta twisters," exhibit the social elements inside their populaces.

   These get-togethers fill different needs, including insurance from hunters, collective searching, and open doors for puppies to cooperate with others. The shared ways of behaving of manta beams stress the interconnectedness of their lives and feature the significance of social associations in their beginning phases of life.

5. **Physiological Transformations and Formative Achievements**

   The physiological transformations of manta beam little guys during their initial days assume a vital part in their endurance. From the snapshot of birth, little guys display ways of behaving that demonstrate their availability for free life, including swimming and searching.

   Formative achievements, for example, the development of their wing range and the obtaining of hunting abilities, mark the movement from weak outset to a stronger stage. Understanding the physiological transformations and formative phases of manta beam puppies gives important bits of knowledge into their capacities and weaknesses during the beginning of life.

6. **Preservation Difficulties and Systems**

The beginning of manta beam puppies harmonize with various protection challenges. Overfishing, territory debasement, and environmental change compromise the sensitive equilibrium of marine biological systems, influencing the accessibility of food assets and presenting puppies to extra dangers.

Protection procedures should address these difficulties exhaustively. Laying out marine safeguarded regions, controlling fishing rehearses, and advancing reasonable the travel industry rehearses are fundamental parts of protecting manta beam populaces during their initial days. Moreover, bringing issues to light about the significance of these maritime goliaths and their weakness during earliest stages adds to worldwide protection endeavors.

In resulting reactions, we can dig further into every one of these perspectives, investigating the particulars of manta beam births, the complexities of maternal consideration, the social elements of early life, physiological variations, and the basic job of protection in guaranteeing a flourishing future for manta beam populaces.

3.1 Birth Process of Manta Ray Pups

The birth interaction of manta beam puppies is an interesting excursion that denotes the finish of a complex and painstakingly organized regenerative cycle. In contrast to a few different elasmobranchs, for example, sharks, manta beams bring forth live and full fledged little guys, revealing a one of a kind part of their conceptive methodology. In this investigation, we dig into the many-sided subtleties of the birth cycle of manta beam little guys, from the commencement of work to the main snapshots of autonomous life in the vast sea.

1. **Commencement of Work: An Exact Organic Occasion**

   The commencement of work in manta beams is an exact natural occasion set off by the fruition of the development time frame. The incubation time frame differs among manta beam species however for the most part goes on for about a year. As the time approaches for birth, the mother goes through hormonal changes that signal the beginning of work.

   The specific triggers for the commencement of work in manta beams are as yet an area of dynamic examination, however it is accepted that hormonal movements assume a huge part. The multifaceted interchange of regenerative chemicals organizes the last phases of growth and readies the mother for the birth cycle.

2. **Determination of Birthing Areas: An Essential Decision**

   Manta beams display a striking level of selectivity with regards to picking birthing areas. While the specific measures for choosing these locales are not completely perceived, there are recognizable examples. Birthing frequently happens in unambiguous regions that give a level of security to both the mother and the infant puppies.

   Shallow seaside regions and reef conditions are ordinarily picked as birthing areas. These locales offer regular hindrances against bigger hunters, establishing a more secure climate for the weak puppies during their initial snapshots of life. The determination of birthing areas highlights the essential decisions made by manta beam moms to improve the possibilities of little guy endurance.

3. **Work and Ejection: The Finish of Incubation**

   The work cycle in manta beams includes the ejection of at least one full grown puppies from the mother's body. This pivotal occasion is a zenith of the growth time frame and denotes the start of another age in the maritime domain.

Work in manta beams is a somewhat quick cycle, and the removal of puppies is worked with by the constrictions of the mother's regenerative lot. The whole work process is a demonstration of the proficiency of manta beam conceptive transformations, guaranteeing that the weak puppies are brought into the world without stretched out openness to expected dangers.

The birthing occasion is definitely not a single event; rather, it frequently includes various puppies being brought into the world in progression. The capacity of manta beam moms to bring forth different little guys during a solitary work occasion adds to the generally conceptive outcome of their populaces.

4. **Qualities of Manta Beam Births: Live and Full fledged Posterity**

One of the unmistakable highlights of manta beam births is the live and full grown nature of the posterity. In contrast to a few different elasmobranchs, where little guys might be brought into the world in a prior transformative phase and go through additional development outside the belly, manta beam puppies are conceived prepared for free life.

The full grown nature of manta beam puppies is a striking variation to their current circumstance. It permits them to participate in fundamental ways of behaving, like swimming and scavenging, expanding their possibilities of endurance during the basic beginning of life right away. The live birth methodology of manta beams mirrors a transformative answer for the difficulties presented by the vast sea climate.

5. **Weaknesses During Birth: Regular Dangers and Human Effects**

While the birth interaction is a wonder of nature, manta beam little guys face weaknesses during this critical period. Regular dangers, for example, predation from bigger marine species like sharks and orcas, represent a consistent gamble. The shallow seaside regions picked for birthing give some security, however the weakness of infant puppies is a reality they should defy.

Human effects further compound the difficulties looked by manta beam puppies during birth. Entrapment in fishing gear, environment debasement, and contamination are huge dangers that can influence the wellbeing and endurance of both mother and posterity. Preservation endeavors should address these difficulties to guarantee the prosperity of manta beam populaces during their weak early days.

6. **Maternal Presence: The Principal Snapshots of Direction**

The job of maternal consideration starts following birth as manta beam moms show an exceptional level of presence and mindfulness of their infant little guys. The mother stays near her posterity, giving security and direction during these underlying minutes in the vast sea.

The maternal presence is vital for the endurance of manta beam puppies, particularly taking into account the variety of potential dangers they might experience. The mother's direction reaches out past the quick post-birth time frame, adding to the improvement of fundamental abilities to survive in her posterity.

7. **Exploring the Untamed Sea: Early Ways of behaving of Manta Beam Puppies**

The early ways of behaving displayed by manta beam puppies are fundamental for their variation to the difficulties of the untamed sea. From the snapshot of birth, little guys participate in natural exercises that set up for their autonomous lives.

Swimming is one of the primary ways of behaving saw in manta beam puppies. The capacity to explore the water segment is vital for their endurance, permitting them to keep away from hunters and search out appropriate natural surroundings. Scrounging ways of behaving likewise arise right off the bat, as little guys investigate and collaborate with their environmental factors looking for food.

These early ways of behaving address a blend of intuition and learned reactions, molded by the direction of the mother and the ecological prompts of the maritime domain. The versatility of manta beam puppies during these underlying stages adds to their strength in the unique marine climate.

8. **The Job of Kin Association: Collective Learning**

Manta beam births frequently include the synchronous rise of different little guys, prompting kin cooperations during their initial days. These connections assume a part in mutual learning, as little guys explore the difficulties of the untamed sea together.

Perceptions of manta beam populaces propose that kin take part in ways of behaving that might work with learning, like agreeable scavenging and social cooperations. The presence of kin during the good 'ol days offers extra help for each little guy, improving their possibilities of endurance in the perplexing marine environment.

9. **Preservation Contemplations: Safeguarding Birth Locales and Weak Little guys**

Preservation endeavors focused on manta beam populaces should focus on the insurance of birthing destinations and the weak little guys during their initial days. Laying out and keeping up with marine safeguarded regions that include these basic areas is fundamental for protecting the conceptive progress of manta beams.

Tending to human-initiated dangers, for example, overfishing, living space corruption, and contamination, is similarly critical. Dependable fishing rehearses, feasible the travel industry, and drives to lessen plastic contamination add to establishing a protected climate for manta beam little guys during their developmental stages.

3.2 Vulnerabilities and Threats during Early Life

The early existence of manta beam little guys is a tricky excursion, loaded up with both normal difficulties and human-prompted dangers. As these effortless marine animals change from the safeguarded climate of incubation to the vast waters of the sea, they experience a horde of weaknesses that can influence their endurance. In this investigation, we dive into the complexities of the weaknesses and dangers looked by manta beam puppies during their pivotal early days, featuring the fragile equilibrium they should explore to flourish in the powerful marine environment.

1. **Normal Dangers: Predation in the Untamed Sea**

   One of the essential normal dangers looked by manta beam puppies during their initial life comes as predation. Regardless of their size and the defensive procedures utilized by their moms, infant manta beam puppies are as yet powerless against bigger marine species that possess the untamed sea. Sharks and orcas, specifically, represent a huge gamble to these youthful marine occupants.

   In the shallow seaside regions and reef conditions picked as birthing areas, manta beam moms look to alleviate the danger of predation by choosing locales with regular boundaries. Be that as it may, as the puppies adventure into more profound waters, the gamble of experiences with ruthless species increments. The beginning of a manta beam little guy's life become a fragile dance between endurance impulses and the consistently present danger of regular hunters.

2. **Human-Prompted Dangers: Ensnarement and Environment Corruption**

   Past the difficulties presented by normal hunters, manta beam little guys face a variety of human-initiated dangers that compound their weaknesses. One of the huge worries is the gamble of trap in fishing gear. As these youthful marine occupants investigate their environmental elements and explore sea flows, they might experience disposed of fishing nets and lines, prompting ensnarement. Entrapment presents serious dangers to manta beam puppies, confining their developments, causing wounds, and, in outrageous cases, prompting fatalities. The issue is exacerbated by the broad utilization of non-particular fishing gear, which may inadvertently catch these delicate monsters alongside target species. Environment debasement further adds to the difficulties looked by manta beam puppies during their initial life. Waterfront advancement, contamination, and environmental change add to the weakening of fundamental living spaces, disturbing the sensitive equilibrium expected for their endurance. Coral reefs, specifically, which act as basic birthing areas, are progressively compromised, influencing the accessibility of appropriate conditions for the weak puppies.

3. **Contamination and Its Consequences: An Approaching Danger**

   Contamination, in different structures, creates a shaded area over the early existence of manta beam little guys. Plastic contamination, specifically, represents a critical danger as it overruns the world's seas. Drifting flotsam and jetsam, like plastic sacks and microplastics, can be confused with prey by manta beam little guys, prompting ingestion and potential unexpected problems.

Synthetic contaminations, including oil slicks and farming overflow, further add to the debasement of water quality in manta beam territories. The repercussions of contamination reach out past prompt actual mischief; they can significantly affect the wellbeing and prosperity of manta beam populaces, remembering interruptions to conceptive achievement and formative anomalies for puppies.

4. **Environmental Change and Sea Fermentation: Disturbing Patterns**

   Environmental change and its related effects, including climbing ocean temperatures and sea fermentation, arise as overall dangers to marine life, including manta beam little guys. The warming of sea waters influences the dispersion of prey species, possibly adjusting the accessibility of food assets for youthful manta beams.

   Sea fermentation, driven by the retention of abundance carbon dioxide via seawater, presents dangers to the improvement of marine creatures, including the planktonic prey that manta beam little guys depend on. The interconnected idea of marine biological systems implies that interruptions at the foundation of the well established pecking order can have flowing impacts, influencing the accessibility and nature of sustenance for weak little guys.

5. **Protection Difficulties: Tending to the Intricate Trap of Dangers**

   The protection challenges related with the weaknesses and dangers looked by manta beam puppies during their initial life are multi-layered. Really tending to these difficulties requires an exhaustive methodology that thinks about both normal and human-incited factors. Protection systems should be versatile and receptive to the advancing elements of marine environments and the rising tensions looked by manta beam populaces.

6. **Relieving Regular Dangers: Understanding Hunter Prey Elements**

   Moderating the regular dangers presented by hunters implies acquiring a more profound comprehension of the intricate elements between manta beam little guys and their expected aggressors. Investigation into the ways of behaving and associations between manta beams and ruthless species can illuminate preservation techniques pointed toward limiting the dangers looked by weak little guys. Key environment the executives, for example, the foundation of marine safeguarded regions that envelop basic birthing locales, assumes an imperative part in lessening the openness of manta beam puppies to normal dangers.

   These safeguarded regions give asylum and permit to the undisturbed improvement of the weak youthful people, adding to the general strength of manta beam populaces.

7. **Tending to Human-Actuated Dangers: Maintainable Fishing Practices**

   Moderating human-initiated dangers requires a deliberate work to advance supportable fishing rehearses and lessen the effect of anthropogenic exercises on manta beam environments. The execution of specific and harmless to the ecosystem fishing gear limits the gamble of entrapment for manta beam puppies and grown-ups the same.

Drawing in with nearby networks and fishing businesses to bring issues to light about the significance of safeguarding manta beams and their living spaces cultivates a feeling of stewardship. Cooperative drives between protection associations, states, and the fishing area can prompt the turn of events and reception of dependable fishing rehearses that focus on the prosperity of marine life.

8. **Plastic Contamination Arrangements: Decreasing the Tide of Garbage**

Tending to the danger of plastic contamination requires a deliberate work to decrease the flood of plastic trash into marine conditions. Public mindfulness crusades, squander the executives drives, and the advancement of choices to single-use plastics add to relieving the effects of plastic contamination on manta beam little guys.

Worldwide coordinated effort is crucial for tackle the worldwide idea of plastic contamination. Systems and arrangements pointed toward lessening plastic creation, further developing waste administration foundation, and advancing reusing can have broad impacts in shielding marine territories and the weak animals that occupy them.

9. **Environmental Change Moderation and Variation: A Worldwide Objective**

The broad effects of environmental change and sea fermentation request worldwide endeavors to alleviate their belongings and adjust to the changing states of marine biological systems. Decrease of ozone harming substance emanations, change to sustainable power sources, and global collaboration on environment related strategies are basic to address the underlying drivers of these dangers.

Nearby transformation procedures, for example, the ID and security of environment versatile living spaces for manta beam puppies, assume a part in improving their possibilities of endurance in an evolving climate. Observing and research endeavors assist with following the impacts of environmental change on manta beam populaces, illuminating versatile administration systems to guarantee their drawn out strength.

10. **Protection Training and Local area Commitment: Encouraging Stewardship**

A fundamental part of protection endeavors is instruction and commitment with nearby networks and the more extensive public. Building mindfulness about the weaknesses and dangers looked by manta beam puppies encourages a feeling of stewardship and aggregate liability regarding the security of these marine animals.

Local area based protection drives, including ecotourism programs that underline mindful practices, add to the economical conjunction of human exercises and manta beam living spaces. By including neighborhood networks in preservation endeavors, there is a chance to make a positive effect on the prosperity of manta beam puppies and their environments.

11. Logical Exploration: Illuminating Preservation Techniques

Logical examination stays a foundation of successful preservation systems for manta beam puppies. Progressing checking of populaces, social examinations, and examinations concerning the natural elements of their living spaces give important bits of knowledge that illuminate versatile administration rehearses.

Coordinated effort between researchers, preservationists, and neighborhood networks upgrades the adequacy of examination drives. The mix of conventional environmental information with logical discoveries makes a comprehensive comprehension of manta beam populaces and their weaknesses, directing preservation activities that are both proof based and socially delicate.

3.3 Maternal Guidance and Protection

In the immense territory of the untamed sea, maternal consideration assumes a vital part in forming the fate of marine life. Among the grand occupants of the ocean, manta beams stand apart for their effortlessness and class as well as for the profundity of maternal direction and security they give to their posterity. This investigation digs into the multifaceted universe of maternal consideration in manta beams, unwinding the subtleties of how moms guide and safeguard their young, adding to the strength and endurance of the cutting edge in the maritime domain.

1. **The Maternal Bond: An Establishment for Endurance**

   The excursion of maternal direction and insurance starts with the foundation of a significant connection between manta beam moms and their posterity. This association is manufactured during incubation, as moms support their creating little guys inside the security of their bodies. The physiological transformations that help this association, for example, the development of a yolk sac placenta, establish the groundwork for the essential job moms play in the existences of their young.

   The maternal bond stretches out past the limits of growth and turns into a foundation of the beginning phases of a manta beam little guy's life. As the snapshot of birth draws near, the mother's impulse to secure and direct her posterity turns out to be progressively obvious, making way for a harmonious relationship that is key to the endurance of these maritime monsters.

2. **Birth and the Main Snapshots of Direction**

   The birthing system itself turns into a demonstration of the maternal responsibility of manta beams. Dissimilar to a few different elasmobranchs, manta beam little guys are conceived live and full fledged, prepared to set out on their free excursion in the untamed sea. The main snapshots of direction from the mother are basic as she guarantees the security and prosperity of her babies in the powerful marine climate.

   The mother's presence during the underlying phases of a little guy's life fills different needs. It gives a feeling that everything is good, permitting the little guy to adapt to its environmental factors and take part in fundamental ways of behaving like swimming and searching. The mother's direction during these developmental minutes is a sensitive dance between encouraging freedom and guaranteeing the little guy's capacity to explore the difficulties of the untamed sea.

3. **Navigational Abilities and Endurance Impulses**

   Maternal direction stretches out to the advancement of pivotal navigational abilities and endurance impulses in manta beam little guys. The vast sea represents a horde of difficulties, and moms assume a key part in conferring the information fundamental for their posterity to flourish. From understanding sea flows to recognizing reasonable living spaces and scavenging grounds, the direction given by moms turns into an outline for the endurance of the future.

   Perceptions of manta beam populaces propose that moms effectively take part in showing their young fundamental abilities. Puppies frequently imitate the ways of behaving of their moms, figuring out how to explore the water segment, stay away from possible dangers, and search out food sources. The exchange of information from mother to little guy adds to the flexibility and strength of manta beam populaces in assorted marine biological systems.

4. **Expanded Maternal Consideration: A Responsibility Past Birth**

   The responsibility of manta beam moms reaches out past the quick post-birth time frame, incorporating a lengthy period of maternal consideration. Dissimilar to species where parental consideration closes not long after birth, manta beams display a wonderful devotion to the prosperity of their posterity. The purposes for this drawn out care are perplexing and complex, mirroring the complicated social elements and methods for surviving of these marine animals.

   During the beginning of a manta beam little guy's life, the mother stays a consistent presence, offering direction and insurance. The sustaining job incorporates establishing a solid climate for the little guy to master fundamental abilities. This drawn out time of maternal consideration adds to the improvement of the little guy's autonomy, guaranteeing confronting the difficulties of the untamed ocean is completely ready.

5. **Kin Connections and Social Elements**

   Manta beams, frequently saw as lone animals, display social elements that incorporate cooperations between kin. Birth occasions frequently include the synchronous rise of various puppies, prompting shared ways of behaving that add to the growth opportunities of the youthful beams. Kin cooperations assume a part in the socialization and variation of manta beam puppies to their maritime climate.

   Perceptions of manta beam populaces have reported ways of behaving like helpful rummaging and composed developments among kin. These connections upgrade the basic instincts of individual puppies and add to the general versatility of manta beam populaces. The social elements inside manta beam families, directed by maternal consideration, highlight the significance of collective learning in the beginning phases of life.

6. **The Job of Maternal Watchfulness: Assurance Against Dangers**

Maternal security is a significant part of manta beam care, particularly during the weak beginning of a little guy's life. The vast sea is overflowing with likely dangers, from normal hunters to human-prompted difficulties, and moms effectively take part in shielding their posterity. Maternal watchfulness turns into a safeguard against the risks that youthful manta beams might experience.

Even with normal dangers, for example, predation from bigger marine species, the mother expects a guarded position, situating herself between possible dangers and her weak little guy. This defensive way of behaving stretches out to human-instigated dangers, including fishing gear snare and territory debasement. Maternal cautiousness is a demonstration of the intuitive responsibility of manta beam moms to the security and prosperity of their posterity.

7. **Preservation Contemplations: Safeguarding Maternal Shelters**

Understanding the significance of maternal direction and insurance is essential to powerful manta beam preservation. Preservation endeavors should focus on the assurance of basic territories where moms conceive an offspring and give stretched out care to their young. Laying out marine safeguarded regions that incorporate these maternal asylums guarantees the conservation of key destinations for manta beam populaces.

Tending to human-instigated dangers, for example, overfishing and environment corruption, is a basic part of manta beam protection. Capable fishing rehearses, maintainable the travel industry, and drives to lessen plastic contamination add to establishing a protected climate for moms and their posterity. Preservation techniques that consider the perplexing interchange of maternal consideration and biological elements are fundamental for the drawn out prosperity of manta beam populaces.

8. **The Crossing point of Science and Protection: Informed Navigation**

Logical exploration assumes a urgent part in unwinding the complexities of maternal direction and security in manta beams. Continuous investigations that screen conceptive ways of behaving, natural surroundings inclinations, and social elements contribute significant bits of knowledge to preservation direction. The incorporation of logical discoveries into preservation methodologies guarantees that drives are proof based and custom fitted to the particular requirements of manta beam populaces.

Cooperation between researchers, moderates, and neighborhood networks upgrades the viability of exploration and protection endeavors. The blend of conventional natural information with logical perceptions gives a comprehensive comprehension of manta beam conduct and environment, working with educated decision-production for the insurance regarding maternal shelters and the prosperity of the future.

9. **Public Mindfulness and Backing: Encouraging Appreciation for Manta Beam Moms**

Public mindfulness and backing drives assume an essential part in earning support for manta beam protection. By featuring the unpredictable maternal consideration showed by these marine goliaths, support endeavors can cultivate a more profound appreciation for the significance of safeguarding their environments and guaranteeing the endurance of people in the future.

Instructive projects, outreach missions, and ecotourism drives that underscore mindful practices add to a worldwide comprehension of the meaning of maternal direction and security in manta beams. Engaging people group and people to become stewards of the sea builds up the aggregate liability to shield the miracles of marine life.

Chapter 4

Growth And Development

In the immense fields of the world's seas, manta beams set out on a noteworthy excursion of development and improvement, unfurling a story that entwines science, biology, and the unique powers of the marine climate. From the snapshot of birth to adulthood, these glorious animals explore the difficulties of the untamed sea, displaying an extraordinary arrangement of transformations that shape their development and characterize their spot in the complicated trap of marine life. This investigation digs into the complexities of development and improvement in manta beams, unwinding the phases of their life cycle and the elements that impact their development into maritime ministers.

1. **The Intrinsic Polish of Manta Beam Births**

   The excursion of development and advancement in manta beams begins with the scene of birth. Not at all like a portion of their elasmobranch family members, manta beam little guys are conceived live and full grown, a stunning occasion that highlights the intrinsic polish of their conceptive procedure. The birthing system, happening in unambiguous waterfront regions and reef conditions, denotes the commencement of the little guy's autonomous life in the vast sea.

   The live birth system of manta beams mirrors a transformative variation to the difficulties of the untamed sea climate. The full fledged nature of the little guys permits them to quickly participate in fundamental ways of behaving, like swimming and searching, upgrading their possibilities of endurance during the basic beginning of life. The birthing occasion fills in as a preface to the unfurling story of development and improvement that will shape the predetermination of every manta beam.

2. **Beginning of Investigation: Exploring the Maritime Domain**

   The beginning of a manta beam little guy's life are portrayed by a time of investigation and transformation. Naturally introduced to the limitlessness of the untamed sea, the little guy starts to explore its environmental elements, directed by maternal consideration and instinctual ways of behaving. Swimming turns into a key expertise, empowering the little guy to cross the water segment and search out reasonable natural surroundings for rummaging and cover.

During this exploratory stage, maternal direction assumes an essential part. The mother stays a consistent presence, giving a safe climate to the little guy to master fundamental abilities.

The flexibility of manta beam puppies during these early days makes way for their development and advancement, as they experience the intricacies of the marine biological system.

3. **Physiological Transformations: The Specialty of Getting by in the Vast Sea**
The development and improvement of manta beams are unpredictably connected to a progression of physiological variations that prepare them for life in the vast sea. One of the characterizing highlights of manta beams is their cephalic balances, which are exceptionally spread out to frame particular "wings." These wings, or pectoral blades, are a sign of their tastefulness as well as fundamental for impetus and mobility.

The cephalic balances, joined with a smoothed out body and a dorsoventrally leveled shape, add to the effective swimming capacities of manta beams. The plan of their gill cuts takes into consideration constant water stream, working with effective oxygen extraction. These physiological variations are sharpened from the beginning of investigation, as manta beam puppies refine their swimming methods and adjust to the requests of the untamed sea climate.

4. **Dietary Changes: From Maternal Milk to Autonomous Rummaging**
As manta beam puppies progress from the maternal consideration stage to free life, a critical part of their development includes dietary changes. In the underlying stages, mother's milk gives fundamental supplements to sustain the little guys. This early eating routine backings their quick development and advancement, permitting them to achieve the actual ability expected for autonomous scrounging.

The change to free rummaging marks a basic achievement in the existence of a manta beam. Puppies start to investigate the maritime domain looking for prey, fundamentally comprising of little fish and planktonic organic entities. The particular cephalic blades, adjusted for productive swimming, assume a critical part in these searching undertakings. The dietary advances of manta beams mirror their ability to adjust to changing nourishing requirements at various phases of development.

5. **Wing Extension and Development: A Visual Ensemble**
The development of manta beams is outwardly enthralling, especially in the extension of their particular wings. The wingspan of manta beams can arrive at amazing extents, for certain people bragging traverses north of 20 feet. This

extension is a demonstration of their development and improvement, as they mature from the little, weak puppies naturally introduced to the world to the radiant, boundless grown-ups that elegance the sea profundities.

The development of their wings isn't exclusively a tasteful peculiarity; it fills a practical need in the existence of manta beams. The extended wings give expanded surface region, supporting effective swimming and coasting through the water.

The visual ensemble of manta beam wing extension typifies the agreement of their development, mirroring the interconnected dance among science and natural transformation.

6. **Sexual Development and Conceptive Availability**

The excursion of development and improvement in manta beams finishes in sexual development, denoting the status for propagation. The age at which manta beams arrive at sexual development can shift among species, commonly happening when people accomplish a specific size and actual development. The fulfillment of sexual development is a groundbreaking stage, molding the conceptive elements and adding to the progression of manta beam populaces.

Manta beams display amazing life span, for certain people living for a considerable length of time. The drawn out life expectancy gives more than adequate chance to development, development, and the aggregation of regenerative experience. Sexual development in manta beams implies the fruition of their formative process and the beginning of another part in their job inside the marine biological system.

7. **The Dance of Romance: An Introduction to Proliferation**

Generation in manta beams includes an enrapturing dance of romance, where people take part in intricate presentations to draw in expected mates. The romance customs are a sign of the mind boggling social elements inside manta beam populaces, giving bits of knowledge into their conduct variations for fruitful propagation.

Male manta beams are known for taking part in aerobatic shows, somersaults, and synchronized swimming to court females. The romance dance works with mate choice as well as fills in for the purpose of correspondence inside the populace. The subtleties of romance customs feature the refinement of manta beam social designs and the interconnectedness of their development, improvement, and conceptive systems.

8. **Generation: Birth and the Continuation of Life's Cycle**

The apex of development and advancement in manta beams is acknowledged in the supernatural course of propagation. Females, having arrived at sexual development, go through incubation, supporting the cutting edge inside their bodies. The development time frame changes among manta beam species, normally going on something like a year. The birthing occasion, set apart by the removal of live and full fledged puppies, goes full circle of propagation, and the pattern of development starts once more.

The regenerative systems of manta beams, including live birth and expanded maternal consideration, add to the endurance and versatility of their populaces. The introduction of new manta beam little guys represents the continuation of life's cycle in the vast sea, with every age acquiring the transformations and ways of behaving fundamental for flourishing in their dynamic marine climate.

9. **Preservation Suggestions: Protecting Development and Improvement**

The preservation of manta beams incorporates the security of their environments, the relief of human-actuated dangers, and the conservation of basic conceptive and scavenging regions. Understanding the complexities of development and advancement in manta beams is necessary to planning successful protection techniques that address the difficulties they face in the cutting edge period.

Territory protection is a foundation of manta beam preservation, guaranteeing the accessibility of reasonable conditions for their development and conceptive exercises. Marine safeguarded regions, intended to envelop key natural surroundings and relocation courses, add to the conservation of fundamental regions for manta beam populaces.

Relieving human-instigated dangers, for example, overfishing, living space debasement, and plastic contamination, is fundamental for protecting the development and improvement of manta beams. Dependable fishing rehearses, economical the travel industry, and local area commitment assume critical parts in lessening the effect of anthropogenic exercises on these marine goliaths.

10. **Logical Exploration: Enlightening the Secrets of Development**

Logical exploration keeps on assuming a critical part in disentangling the secrets of development and improvement in manta beams. Progressing studies into their conceptive science, transient examples, and hereditary variety give important bits of knowledge into their life history and add to confirm based protection measures.

Coordinated effort between researchers, moderates, and nearby networks upgrades the viability of examination drives. The combination of customary natural information with logical discoveries makes a comprehensive comprehension of manta beam populaces, revealing insight into the elements impacting their development and improvement.

11. **Instruction and Effort: Cultivating Appreciation for Manta Beams**

Instructive drives and effort programs are fundamental for encouraging appreciation for the development and improvement of manta beams. By bringing issues to light about their life history, biological significance, and the difficulties they face, these projects add to a worldwide comprehension of the meaning of protecting these marine representatives.

Ecotourism, when drilled dependably, gives a road to people to observe the gloriousness of manta beams right at home. This firsthand experience cultivates an association among individuals and marine life, moving a feeling of stewardship and a promise to the protection of these enamoring animals.

4.1 Feeding Habits and Diet of Manta Ray Pups

In the purplish blue territories of the world's seas, manta beam puppies set out on a culinary excursion that shapes their development, improvement, and endurance. The taking care of propensities and diet of these youthful marine occupants are a demonstration of the complexities of their natural specialty and the interconnected snare of life in the maritime domain. This investigation digs into the captivating universe of what, when, and how manta beam puppies eat, disentangling the subtleties of their taking care of ways of behaving and dietary inclinations as they explore the huge blue territory.

1. **Birth and Early Sustenance: A Brief look into Maternal Milk**

   The culinary excursion of manta beam little guys starts with the novel peculiarity of live birth. Not at all like their shark family members, manta beam little guys are conceived full fledged and prepared for the difficulties of the vast sea. In their initial days, sustenance comes as maternal milk, a striking variation that gives fundamental supplements to fast development and improvement.

   Maternal milk fills in as a concentrated wellspring of energy, proteins, and fats, outfitting the little guys with the fundamental assets to progress from the safeguarded climate of development to the extensive and dynamic universe of the vast sea. The milk gives a dietary establishment that upholds the underlying phases of investigation, swimming, and searching, making way for the continuous change to free taking care of.

2. **Progress to Autonomy: Scrounging in the Vast Sea**

   As manta beam little guys develop and create, the change to free taking care of imprints a significant stage in their culinary excursion. This progress is described by a change in dietary inclinations and scavenging techniques, as the little guys investigate the boundlessness of their maritime climate looking for food.

   Manta beam puppies fundamentally feed on planktonic creatures, including little fish, shellfish, and minuscule zooplankton. Their rummaging conduct is described by effortless swimming, frequently close to the sea's surface, where centralizations of microscopic fish are more bountiful. The particular cephalic blades, which give manta beams their unmistakable appearance, assume a vital part in coordinating microscopic fish rich water towards their mouths, considering proficient channel taking care of.

3. **Channel Taking care of Elements: Tackling the Force of Water**

   The taking care of propensities for manta beam puppies are exemplified by their ability in channel taking care of. This strategy includes the ingestion of huge volumes of water, from which planktonic prey is sifted through utilizing specific gill rakers. The separating system is worked with by the mind boggling design of the gill contraption, which permits water to go through while holding prey things.

Manta beams are known for their aerobatic taking care of showcases, especially close to the sea's surface where tiny fish fixations are higher. The broad developments of their cephalic blades make a pipe like impact, directing water into their mouths. As the water goes through their gill rakers, planktonic living beings are caught and consequently drank. This channel taking care of methodology is a demonstration of the biological flexibility of manta beams, permitting them to flourish in different maritime conditions.

4. **Dietary Inclinations: A Planktonic Undertaking**

The eating regimen of manta beam little guys rotates around the rich woven artwork of planktonic life in the untamed sea. Tiny fish, including both phytoplankton (minuscule plants) and zooplankton (infinitesimal creatures), frames the foundation of their culinary inclinations. The different cluster of planktonic life forms fills in as an essential wellspring of nourishment, adding to the enthusiastic requests of their quick development and improvement.

Manta beam puppies show adaptability in their dietary inclinations, benefiting from an assortment of planktonic prey. Little fish, larval phases of scavangers, and different kinds of zooplankton become staple parts of their eating routine. This flexibility permits manta beam little guys to flourish in various maritime locales, where the piece of planktonic networks might change.

5. **Natural Impacts: Exploring Tiny fish Blossoms**

The taking care of propensities for manta beam puppies are unpredictably connected to natural impacts, with the accessibility of microscopic fish being a critical determinant of their searching achievement. Tiny fish sprouts, described by an overflow of infinitesimal creatures, make ideal circumstances for manta beam taking care of. These sprouts can happen because of occasional changes, supplement upwelling, and oceanographic highlights that concentrate planktonic life.

Manta beams show a degree of natural mindfulness in their scrounging ways of behaving, frequently congregating in regions where microscopic fish fixations are high. The capacity to explore and take advantage of microscopic fish blossoms is a powerful part of their taking care of biology, permitting them to profit by the transient and spatially factor nature of their essential food source.

6. **Occasional and Geographic Changeability: Adjusting to Changing Circumstances**

The culinary excursion of manta beam little guys is certainly not a static undertaking yet rather one portrayed by versatility to evolving conditions. Occasional and geographic changeability in maritime conditions impact the appropriation and wealth of planktonic prey, provoking manta beams to adjust their searching ways of behaving because of these vacillations.

In certain locales, manta beams might display transient examples looking for ideal scrounging grounds. The quest for planktonic overflow drives these developments, mirroring the powerful interaction between the culinary necessities of manta beam puppies and the always changing states of the untamed sea. Such versatility is a demonstration of the strength imbued in their taking care of systems.

7. **Social Scavenging: People group Elements in Culinary Pursuits**
   Manta beams, frequently saw as singular animals, participate in friendly scrounging ways of behaving that add a layer of intricacy to their culinary excursion. While scrounging is principally a singular pursuit, accumulations of manta beams are ordinarily seen in areas of plentiful tiny fish. These collections lead to social connections, with various people joining in a common quest for culinary joys.

   Social rummaging among manta beams isn't completely perceived, yet perceptions recommend that conglomerations might give advantages like expanded scavenging proficiency, hunter evasion, and correspondence of ideal searching circumstances. The elements of social connections with regards to scavenging add to the more extensive comprehension of manta beam local area structures and their job in the marine environment.

8. **Anthropogenic Impacts: Exploring Human-Prompted Difficulties**
   While manta beam little guys have developed to explore the powerful difficulties of the vast sea, human-instigated impacts represent a huge danger to their culinary excursion. Overfishing, territory debasement, and environmental change can disturb the sensitive equilibrium of planktonic biological systems, influencing the accessibility of fundamental prey things for manta beams.

   One striking anthropogenic impact is plastic contamination, which inescapably affects marine conditions. Planktonic organic entities might confuse microplastics with food, prompting bioaccumulation of toxins in their tissues. As manta beam little guys channel feed on tiny fish, there is an expected gamble of ingesting microplastics, with likely ramifications for their wellbeing and prosperity.

9. **Preservation Suggestions: Protecting the Culinary Delight**
   Understanding the taking care of propensities and diet of manta beam puppies is basic to forming successful preservation methodologies that address the difficulties they face in the cutting edge period. Preservation drives should focus on the assurance of basic environments, the alleviation of human-prompted dangers, and the safeguarding of planktonic biological systems that structure the groundwork of their culinary excursion.

10. **Marine Safeguarded Regions: Places of refuge for Culinary Investigation**
    Laying out marine safeguarded regions (MPAs) that envelop key natural

surroundings and scavenging grounds is an essential move toward defending the culinary investigation of manta beam little guys. These safeguarded zones give a safe-haven where they can participate in regular scavenging ways of behaving without the quick dangers presented by overfishing, living space debasement, and other anthropogenic impacts.

Planning MPAs with an emphasis on the unique idea of planktonic environments guarantees the protection of fundamental scrounging regions. The outline of these region requires a comprehension of the occasional and geographic fluctuation in microscopic fish blossoms, considering versatile administration procedures that line up with the culinary necessities of manta beam puppies.

11. **Supportable Fisheries The executives: Adjusting Human Requirements and Culinary Agreement**

    Adjusting the culinary requirements of manta beam little guys with human exercises is a fragile errand that requires reasonable fisheries the board. Executing dependable fishing rehearses, for example, keeping away from the utilization of damaging stuff and limiting bycatch, adds to keeping up with sound planktonic environments that help manta beam scrounging.

    Local area commitment assumes a significant part in practical fisheries the board, encouraging a feeling of stewardship and shared liability regarding the marine climate. Cooperative endeavors between nearby networks, researchers, and policymakers add to the improvement of fisheries the executives methodologies that focus on the biological prosperity of marine environments and the culinary amicability of manta beam puppies.

12. **Environmental Change Moderation: Saving Planktonic Overflow**

    The effects of environmental change, including sea warming and fermentation, can have flowing consequences for planktonic biological systems. Alleviating environmental change is fundamental for safeguarding the overflow and variety of tiny fish, which structure the foundation of manta beam little guy counts calories. Worldwide endeavors to diminish fossil fuel byproducts and address environmental change add to the drawn out conservation of their culinary assets.

13. **Public Mindfulness and Training: Sustaining Culinary Appreciation**

    Public mindfulness and schooling drives assume a significant part in encouraging appreciation for the culinary excursion of manta beam little guys.

    By featuring their taking care of propensities, dietary inclinations, and the difficulties they face, these drives add to a worldwide comprehension of the meaning of protecting marine biological systems and the biodiversity they support.

    Instructive projects, outreach missions, and ecotourism drives that underline dependable practices add to a more profound appreciation for the interconnectedness of culinary elements in the sea. Enabling people to become advocates for marine preservation supports the aggregate liability to defend the culinary concordance of manta beam little guys and the more extensive marine climate.

14. Logical Exploration: Enlightening Culinary Secrets

Logical examination stays a foundation in disentangling the secrets of the taking care of propensities and diet of manta beam little guys. Continuous investigations into their scrounging ways of behaving, dietary inclinations, and reactions to ecological changes contribute important bits of knowledge to protection direction. The combination of logical discoveries into preservation procedures guarantees that drives are proof based and customized to the particular culinary necessities of manta beam populaces.

4.2 Developmental Stages: From Pup to Juvenile

The excursion of manta beams from little guy to adolescent is an enamoring story that unfurls in the immense spread of the world's seas. These maritime drifters, naturally introduced to the unique domain of the untamed ocean, go through a progression of formative stages that shape their development, conduct, and step by step processes for surviving. This investigation digs into the unpredictable embroidered artwork of manta beam advancement, following the development from weak little guys to strong adolescents as they explore the difficulties of the marine climate.

1. **Birth and Early Days: The Introduction to Freedom**
   The formative odyssey of manta beams begins with the pivotal occasion of live birth. Not at all like numerous different elasmobranchs, manta beam little guys are conceived full grown and equipped for guaranteed autonomy. The birthing system regularly happens in unambiguous seaside regions and reef conditions, where the mother gives security and direction during the beginning of a little guy's life.

   In the underlying minutes post-birth, the puppies depend on maternal consideration and sustenance, exploiting the supplement rich maternal milk given by their moms. This early period fills in as an essential starting point for their development and sets them up for the possible progress to an existence of freedom in the untamed sea.

2. **Progress to Freedom: Exploring the Vast Sea**
   The progress from little guy to adolescent denotes a critical change in the formative direction of manta beams. As they bid goodbye to the limits of maternal consideration, the little guys start to investigate the limitlessness of the untamed sea. This stage is portrayed by a time of transformation, investigation, and the improving of fundamental endurance abilities.

   During this change, manta beam little guys refine their abilities to swim and scavenging strategies. The unmistakable cephalic balances, which give manta beams their notable appearance, assume a vital part in moving through the water section. As they explore the powerful maritime climate, the little guys steadily become skilled at finding reasonable natural surroundings, recognizing prey, and staying away from possible dangers.

3. **Physiological Variations: Forming the Future Swimmers**
The formative phases of manta beams are joined by a progression of physiological transformations that shape their ability to flourish in the untamed sea. The smoothed out body, combined with the novel construction of their pectoral balances, works with effective swimming and mobility. These transformations, sharpened during the progress from little guy to adolescent, add to the astounding tastefulness and spryness that characterize manta beams in their grown-up stages.

   One of the outstanding physiological transformations is the capacity to effectively channel feed. As adolescents refine their searching methods, the sifting components in their gill rakers permit them to profit by planktonic overflow in the untamed sea. The improvement of these variations is a demonstration of the developmental techniques that empower manta beams to explore their maritime living spaces with elegance and accuracy.

4. **Social Elements: Investigating the Local area Embroidery**
Manta beams, frequently saw as singular animals, show captivating social elements during their formative stages. As adolescents, they might shape accumulations in regions plentiful with food assets, participating in public searching ways of behaving. These social associations add to the trading of data, the improvement of navigational abilities, and the support of endurance impulses.

   The social texture woven during the adolescent stage sets the preparation for the perplexing local area elements saw in grown-up manta beam populaces. These social connections, whether chasing after prey or the aversion of hunters, represent the versatility and cooperative nature of manta beams as they progress through their formative stages.

5. **Dietary Advances: From Maternal Milk to Free Searching**
The change from little guy to adolescent involves a change in dietary inclinations and scrounging systems. While maternal milk gives vital sustenance in the good 'ol days, adolescents progressively make the change to free scavenging. This shift is set apart by an investigation of assorted prey things, including little fish, shellfish, and different sorts of planktonic living beings.

   Adolescent manta beams show adaptability in their dietary decisions, adjusting to the occasional and geographic changeability of planktonic biological systems. The capacity to expand their eating regimen adds to their strength in various maritime conditions, mirroring the versatile idea of their formative stages.

6. **Development and Size Elements: Disclosing Maritime Goliaths really taking shape**
The excursion from little guy to adolescent is joined by critical development and size elements. While brought into the world with noteworthy wingspans,

adolescent manta beams go through significant development as they progress through their formative stages. The development of their pectoral blades adds to their rising wingspan, uncovering the potential for these maritime drifters to become goliaths of the untamed ocean.

Perceptions of adolescent manta beams uncover varieties in size among people, affected by variables like hereditary qualities, natural circumstances, and dietary examples. The development elements of adolescents offer experiences into the many-sided interchange of natural and ecological variables that shape what's in store components of these grand marine animals.

7. **Social Variations: Flourishing in the Vast Sea**

The social variations of manta beams during their formative stages are vital for flourishing in the vast sea. As adolescents, they show a mix of exploratory ways of behaving and wary reactions to possible dangers. The authority of swimming methods, coordination in friendly collaborations, and the refinement of scrounging abilities add to their capacity to explore the tremendous and dynamic marine climate.

One eminent conduct variation is the advancement of navigational abilities that permit adolescent manta beams to cross huge distances looking for ideal scavenging grounds. The capacity to explore the maritime scope mirrors a mix of inborn impulses and gained ways of behaving obtained during their formative process from little guy to adolescent.

8. **Dangers and Weaknesses: Exploring Hazards in Beginning phases**

The formative phases of manta beams, especially from little guy to adolescent, are not without difficulties and weaknesses. Normal hunters, for example, enormous sharks and orcas, present dangers to adolescent manta beams.

Moreover, human-actuated difficulties, remembering entrapment for fishing gear, environment debasement, and environmental change, intensify the dangers looked during these beginning phases of advancement.

The weakness of adolescent manta beams stresses the significance of preservation endeavors to alleviate dangers and safeguard basic natural surroundings. Understanding the environmental elements and conduct transformations of manta beams during their formative stages illuminates protection procedures pointed toward defending these maritime marvels in their early stages.

9. **Protection Contemplations: Defending the Eventual fate of Maritime Monsters**

Preservation drives assume a crucial part in guaranteeing the fruitful change of manta beams from little guy to adolescent and then some. Safeguarding basic environments, carrying out economical fisheries the board rehearses, and tending to anthropogenic dangers are necessary parts of preservation systems for these marine animals.

Marine safeguarded regions (MPAs) that include key formative environments give safe-havens where adolescent manta beams can flourish without quick dangers. Planning MPAs with an emphasis on the formative necessities of manta beams adds to the safeguarding of fundamental regions for their development and development.

10. Examination and Training: Enlightening Formative Secrets

Logical examination keeps on enlightening the secrets of manta beam improvement, revealing insight into their social, physiological, and biological transformations during the change from little guy to adolescent. Progressing studies contribute important bits of knowledge to the comprehension of their life history, local area elements, and communications with the marine climate.

Training drives that feature the formative phases of manta beams cultivate appreciation for these maritime marvels. By bringing issues to light about their weakness during beginning phases and the significance of preservation, instructive projects add to a worldwide comprehension of the need to safeguard the fate of these magnificent marine goliaths.

4.3 Interactions with the Environment and Other Marine Life

Manta beams, as great occupants of the vast sea, take part in captivating communications with their current circumstance and other marine life, winding around a powerful embroidery inside the perplexing trap of marine environments. These associations are essential components of their regular routines, affecting way of behaving, searching techniques, and, surprisingly, adding to the protection of their species.

In their current circumstance, manta beams show a sharp feeling of spatial mindfulness, exploring immense maritime spans looking for ideal scrounging grounds and mating regions. Their connections with sea flows, thermoclines, and submerged geology feature their versatility to the steadily changing marine scene.

Social elements likewise assume a critical part in the existences of manta beams. While frequently saw as lone creatures, they sporadically structure collections, cultivating collaborations with conspecifics during romance presentations or common taking care of. These social experiences give bits of knowledge into the mind boggling correspondence and conduct signs that shape manta beam populaces.

Past their own sort, manta beams connect with a different cluster of marine life. Cleaning stations, where more modest fish assist with eliminating parasites from their skin, epitomize advantageous connections that benefit the two players. Also, the presence of manta beams has biological ramifications, impacting the conveyance and overflow of planktonic life forms, further highlighting their job as cornerstone species in the marine climate. These complex collaborations feature the interconnectedness of manta beams with the maritime domain, improving the biodiversity and natural equilibrium of the world underneath the waves.

Chapter 5

Conservation Challenges

Manta beams, these delicate monsters of the maritime domain, face a heap of preservation challenges that compromise their reality and the sensitive equilibrium of marine biological systems. From anthropogenic tensions to natural changes, understanding and tending to these difficulties are principal for the conservation of these magnetic animals. This investigation digs into the perplexing scene of protection challenges confronting manta beams, revealing insight into the dire requirement for deliberate endeavors to guarantee their endurance in the seas they call home.

1. **Overfishing and Bycatch: An Approaching Danger**
   One of the essential difficulties facing manta beams is overfishing and accidental catch, generally known as bycatch. Manta beams, pursued for their gill plates in conventional medication and their worth in global exchange, succumb to designated fishing and are in many cases caught in nets set for different species. The interest for their body parts, energized by social convictions and business interests, puts tremendous strain on manta beam populaces.
   The result of overfishing reaches out past the immediate effect on manta beams. As channel feeders, they assume a basic part in keeping up with the environmental equilibrium by controlling tiny fish populaces. The decrease in manta beam numbers upsets this equilibrium, possibly prompting flowing impacts on the whole marine food web. Protection endeavors should address the underlying drivers of overfishing and execute measures to diminish bycatch, defending manta beams and the biological systems they occupy.

2. **Environment Corruption and Misfortune: Decreasing Places of refuge**
   Manta beams depend on unambiguous environments for taking care of, mating, and conceiving an offspring. Beach front regions, coral reefs, and useful maritime zones act as fundamental conditions for different life phases of manta beams. In any case, these environments are progressively compromised by human exercises, including waterfront improvement, contamination, and

environmental change.

The corruption of waterfront territories, like mangroves and estuaries, denies manta beams of basic nurseries for their puppies. Coral reefs, essential to their scavenging and cleaning ways of behaving, face dangers from increasing ocean temperatures, coral fading, and horrendous fishing rehearses. The deficiency of these environments straightforwardly influences manta beams as well as upsets the many-sided equilibrium of marine biological systems.

Preservation systems should focus on natural surroundings security, reclamation, and economical improvement practices to give places of refuge to manta beams to flourish.

3. **Environmental Change and Sea Fermentation: A Worldwide Threat**

The ghost of environmental change and sea fermentation represents a dismal danger to manta beam populaces. Increasing ocean temperatures upset the dissemination of microscopic fish, an essential food hotspot for manta beams, possibly modifying their rummaging examples and movement courses. Changes in maritime circumstances can likewise influence the conceptive outcome of manta beams, influencing the accessibility of appropriate regions for development and pupping.

Sea fermentation, driven by the assimilation of abundance carbon dioxide via seawater, further mixtures the difficulties. This peculiarity presents dangers to the soundness of planktonic networks, possibly reducing the essential prey of manta beams. The intensifying impacts of environmental change and sea fermentation highlight the requirement for worldwide drives to moderate fossil fuel byproducts, adjust to evolving conditions, and safeguard manta beam natural surroundings.

4. **Contamination: A Quiet Threat Underneath the Waves**

Marine contamination, going from plastic garbage to synthetic impurities, represents a quiet hazard to manta beams and the marine environments they possess. Ingestion of plastics, frequently confused with prey things, can prompt interior wounds, blockages, and lack of healthy sustenance in manta beams. The steady presence of poisons in their natural surroundings raises worries about the drawn out influences on their wellbeing and conceptive achievement.

Contamination likewise stretches out to substance pollutants, including oil slicks and horticultural overflow, which can poisonously affect manta beams and their prey. As channel feeders, manta beams are helpless against aggregating poisons present in the water, further featuring the requirement for exhaustive waste administration, stricter guidelines, and public mindfulness missions to decrease contamination in marine conditions.

5. **Impractical The travel industry Works on: Adjusting Protection and Monetary Interests**

The ascent of marine the travel industry, energized by the charm of experiencing magnetic species like manta beams, presents a blade that cuts both ways for their protection. While dependable the travel industry can add to mindfulness, subsidizing, and nearby economies, the unregulated development of this industry can prompt unfortunate results for manta beam populaces.

Unreasonable the travel industry rehearses, for example, close and nosy cooperations with manta beams, can upset their normal ways of behaving, cause pressure, and effect conceptive achievement. Besides, the actual presence of boats, clamor contamination, and living space aggravation related with the travel industry exercises can aggregately affect manta beam territories.

Adjusting the monetary advantages of the travel industry with preservation goals requires executing and upholding rules for capable untamed life seeing, laying out marine safeguarded regions, and encouraging local area commitment. Cooperative endeavors between the travel industry, neighborhood networks, and preservation associations are fundamental to guarantee that travel industry turns into a power for positive change as opposed to a danger to manta beam populaces.

6. **Absence of Worldwide Participation: Spanning Holes for Worldwide Protection**

   Manta beams are exceptionally transitory species, navigating global waters and crossing jurisdictional limits. The absence of facilitated worldwide endeavors and bound together protection techniques compounds the difficulties looked by manta beams. Errors in guidelines, requirement components, and information sharing upset viable protection the board.

   Worldwide collaboration is fundamental for the preservation of manta beams, as their endurance relies upon the wellbeing of interconnected maritime environments. Cooperative drives, like the Show on Transitory Species (CMS) and territorial fisheries the executives associations, can assume an essential part in encouraging collaboration, sharing logical information, and laying out protection estimates that rise above public boundaries.

7. **Logical Information Holes: Enlightening the Shadows**

   Notwithstanding developing interest and examination endeavors, there are as yet critical holes in logical information in regards to the environment, conduct, and populace elements of manta beams. Figuring out their transient examples, conceptive science, and availability between populaces is pivotal for creating designated protection techniques.

   The restricted accessibility of extensive information presents difficulties for proof based navigation and the successful execution of protection measures. Crossing over these information holes requires supported research endeavors, mechanical advancements, and coordinated effort between researchers, traditionalists, and nearby networks. By unwinding the secrets of manta beams, mainstream researchers can give basic bits of knowledge that illuminate protection activities and strategy improvement.

8. **Absence of Legitimate Insurances: Upholding for Regulative Protections**
While certain nations have done whatever it takes to safeguard manta beams through public regulation, a worldwide structure for their preservation is inadequate. Manta beams are not covered by peaceful accords that explicitly address their preservation needs. The shortfall of legitimate assurances at the worldwide level leaves them defenseless against double-dealing and inadequate preservation endeavors.

   Backing for the consideration of manta beams in global preservation arrangements, for example, the Show on Worldwide Exchange Jeopardized Types of Wild Fauna and Vegetation (Refers to), is fundamental. Lawful shields can give an establishment to composed preservation activities, work with subsidizing for exploration and insurance drives, and add to bringing issues to light about the significance of manta beam protection on a worldwide scale.

9. **Local area Commitment and Strengthening: Building Nearby Stewardship**
Fruitful protection drives should be established in the commitment and strengthening of neighborhood networks. In numerous districts, manta beams hold social importance, and neighborhood networks frequently assume an essential part in their protection. Boosting maintainable works on, giving elective occupations, and encouraging a feeling of stewardship among local area individuals are key parts of successful protection methodologies.

   Local area based drives, for example, ecotourism programs that focus on dependable practices, contribute not exclusively to the prosperity of manta beams yet in addition to the financial thriving of nearby networks. Building associations between protection associations, state run administrations, and native networks guarantees that preservation endeavors line up with the necessities and goals of the individuals who share their surroundings with manta beams.

10. **Protection Examples of overcoming adversity: Motivation for What's in store**
In spite of the various difficulties confronting manta beams, there are rousing examples of overcoming adversity that deal expectation and direction for what's to come. Nations like Indonesia and Ecuador have executed severe insurances for manta beams, remembering boycotts for fishing and exchange. These protection measures have prompted expansions in manta beam populaces, exhibiting the positive effect of designated mediations.

    Protection examples of overcoming adversity highlight the significance of proactive and science-based approaches. By gaining from these accomplishments, policymakers, progressives, and networks can embrace systems that have demonstrated compelling in protecting manta beams and their environments.

11. **Instructive Drives: Encouraging a Protection Ethos**

Instructive drives are essential to cultivating a preservation ethos that rises above ages. Bringing issues to light about the natural significance of manta beams, the difficulties they face, and the job of people in their protection is fundamental. Schools, people group associations, and online stages can act as incredible assets for scattering data and rousing activity.

Public commitment drives, including narratives, outreach projects, and resident science projects, add to building a worldwide local area of backers for manta beam protection. By imparting a feeling of obligation and love for these marine miracles, instructive endeavors make ready for a future where manta beams flourish in solid seas.

5.1Human Threats and Conservation Challenges

Manta beams, these grand maritime vagabonds, face a variety of human-instigated dangers and preservation challenges that jeopardize their reality and the fragile environments they possess. From designated fishing to environment corruption, the effect of anthropogenic exercises resonates through the immense spread of the world's seas. This far reaching investigation digs into the mind boggling snare of human dangers and protection challenges confronting manta beams, underlining the basic requirement for cooperative and purposeful endeavors to get their future in the marine domain.

1. **Designated Fishing and Bycatch: The Quiet Chase**

   One of the most squeezing dangers to manta beams is designated fishing, driven by the interest for their gill plates in customary Chinese medication and the global exchange of manta beam items. The charm of these cartilaginous monsters has prompted tenacious hunting, pushing a few manta beam animal groups towards the verge of risk.

   Manta beams, frequently got as bycatch in fishing gear planned for different species, experience extra tensions. The aimless idea of specific fishing techniques, for example, gillnets and tote seines, improves the probability of manta beam snare. The outcomes stretch out past the designated people, affecting whole populaces and the complicated equilibrium of marine environments.

   Preservation endeavors should focus on the relief of designated fishing and bycatch through the execution of severe guidelines, checking components, and the advancement of feasible fishing rehearses. Local area commitment and mindfulness crusades are instrumental in changing perspectives towards these maritime goliaths, cultivating a feeling of obligation and upholding for their security.

2. **Territory Corruption and Waterfront Advancement: Upsetting Safe-havens**

   Manta beams depend on unambiguous territories for taking care of, mating, and pupping, and large numbers of these basic regions are under danger because of environment debasement and seaside improvement. Beach front zones, including mangroves and estuaries, act as nurseries for manta beam little guys, giving sanctuary and bountiful food assets. Be that as it may, fast waterfront improvement, driven by urbanization and the travel industry, brings about living space misfortune and corruption, risking the endurance of these weak stages.

Coral reefs, fundamental for manta beam scavenging and cleaning ways of behaving, face debasement from contamination, environmental change, and disastrous fishing rehearses. The deficiency of these territories disturbs manta beam populaces as well as compromises the uprightness of whole marine biological systems.

Preservation techniques should address the underlying drivers of environment debasement, underlining manageable beach front improvement rehearses, marine spatial preparation, and the foundation of marine safeguarded regions (MPAs). These drives plan to defend basic territories and give safe-havens where manta beams can flourish without the quick dangers presented by human exercises.

3. **Environmental Change and Sea Fermentation: A Worldwide Danger Escalates**

Environmental change, filled by anthropogenic exercises, represents an imposing test to manta beams and marine biological systems at large. Climbing ocean temperatures change the dissemination of microscopic fish, an essential food hotspot for manta beams, possibly influencing their scavenging examples and relocation courses. The noteworthy changes in maritime circumstances additionally impact the conceptive progress of manta beams, influencing the accessibility of reasonable regions for development and pupping.

Sea fermentation, driven by the assimilation of overabundance carbon dioxide, represents extra dangers. This peculiarity can upset the soundness of planktonic networks, possibly reducing the essential prey of manta beams. The intensifying impacts of environmental change and sea fermentation feature the interconnectedness of natural difficulties and the requirement for worldwide drives to alleviate fossil fuel byproducts, adjust to evolving conditions, and safeguard manta beam living spaces.

4. **Contamination: A Quiet Intrusion of Marine Domains**

Marine contamination, originating from different sources like plastic garbage, synthetic pollutants, and oil slicks, penetrates the living spaces of manta beams, presenting quiet however inescapable dangers. Ingestion of plastics by manta beams, frequently confused with prey things, can prompt interior wounds, blockages, and lack of healthy sustenance. The steady presence of poisons in their territories raises worries about the drawn out influences on their wellbeing and regenerative achievement.

Compound impurities, including oil slicks and farming spillover, bring poisons into the marine climate. As channel feeders, manta beams are powerless against collecting these toxins in their tissues, raising worries about the potential wellbeing influences on these alluring maritime occupants.

Preservation endeavors should focus on extensive waste administration, stricter guidelines on poison releases, and public mindfulness missions to decrease contamination in marine conditions. Drives, for example, ocean side clean-ups, reusing programs, and the improvement of eco-accommodating choices add to alleviating the effect of contamination on manta beams and their territories.

5. **Unreasonable The travel industry Works on: Adjusting Preservation and Business**

The charm of experiencing manta beams right at home has filled a flood in marine the travel industry, introducing the two open doors and difficulties for their protection. While capable the travel industry can add to mindfulness, financing, and neighborhood economies, the unregulated development of this industry can prompt adverse results for manta beam populaces.

Impractical the travel industry works on, including close and meddlesome cooperations with manta beams, can disturb their regular ways of behaving, cause pressure, and effect conceptive achievement. The actual presence of boats, commotion contamination, and environment aggravation related with the travel industry exercises can in total affect manta beam territories.

Adjusting the financial advantages of the travel industry with preservation goals requires carrying out and implementing rules for dependable untamed life seeing, laying out marine safeguarded regions (MPAs), and encouraging local area commitment. Cooperative endeavors between the travel industry, nearby networks, and preservation associations are fundamental to guarantee that travel industry turns into a power for positive change instead of a danger to manta beam populaces.

6. **Absence of Worldwide Collaboration: Spanning Holes for Worldwide Preservation**

Manta beams are profoundly transitory species, navigating worldwide waters and crossing jurisdictional limits. The absence of composed worldwide endeavors and brought together protection systems fuels the difficulties looked by manta beams. Disparities in guidelines, implementation systems, and information sharing upset successful protection the board.

Worldwide collaboration is fundamental for the preservation of manta beams, as their endurance relies upon the strength of interconnected maritime biological systems.

Cooperative drives, like the Show on Transient Species (CMS) and provincial fisheries the executives associations, can assume a vital part in encouraging collaboration, sharing logical information, and laying out protection estimates that rise above public boundaries.

7. **Logical Information Holes: Enlightening the Shadows**

In spite of developing interest and exploration endeavors, there are as yet huge holes in logical information with respect to the nature, conduct, and populace elements of manta beams. Grasping their transient examples, regenerative science, and availability between populaces is pivotal for creating designated preservation systems.

The restricted accessibility of far reaching information presents difficulties for proof based direction and the powerful execution of preservation measures. Spanning these information holes requires supported research endeavors, mechanical developments, and joint effort between researchers, protectionists, and nearby networks. By disentangling the secrets of manta beams, established researchers can give basic bits of knowledge that illuminate preservation activities and strategy improvement.

8. **Absence of Lawful Securities: Pushing for Authoritative Shields**

While certain nations have done whatever it takes to safeguard manta beams through public regulation, a worldwide system for their protection is deficient. Manta beams are not covered by peaceful accords that explicitly address their protection needs. The shortfall of lawful securities at the global level leaves them powerless against abuse and inadequate protection endeavors.

Promotion for the consideration of manta beams in worldwide preservation arrangements, for example, the Show on Global Exchange Jeopardized Types of Wild Fauna and Verdure (Refers to), is fundamental. Lawful shields can give an establishment to composed preservation activities, work with financing for examination and insurance drives, and add to bringing issues to light about the significance of manta beam protection on a worldwide scale.

9. **Local area Commitment and Strengthening: Building Nearby Stewardship**

Effective protection drives should be established in the commitment and strengthening of nearby networks. In numerous districts, manta beams hold social importance, and neighborhood networks frequently assume a pivotal part in their protection. Boosting economical works on, giving elective occupations, and encouraging a feeling of stewardship among local area individuals are key parts of viable protection procedures.

Local area based drives, for example, ecotourism programs that focus on capable practices, contribute not exclusively to the prosperity of manta beams yet additionally to the financial flourishing of neighborhood networks.

Building associations between preservation associations, state run administrations, and native networks guarantees that protection endeavors line up with the necessities and desires of the people who share their surroundings with manta beams.

10. **Preservation Examples of overcoming adversity: Motivation for What's in store**

Notwithstanding the various difficulties confronting manta beams, there are motivating examples of overcoming adversity that deal expectation and direction for what's in store. Nations like Indonesia and Ecuador have executed severe insurances for manta beams, remembering boycotts for fishing and exchange. These preservation measures have prompted expansions in manta beam populaces, exhibiting the positive effect of designated mediations.

Protection examples of overcoming adversity highlight the significance of proactive and science-based approaches. By gaining from these accomplishments, policymakers, preservationists, and networks can embrace systems that have demonstrated viable in defending manta beams and their living spaces.

11. **Instructive Drives: Encouraging a Protection Ethos**

Instructive drives are necessary to encouraging a preservation ethos that rises above ages. Bringing issues to light about the environmental significance of manta beams, the difficulties they face, and the job of people in their preservation is fundamental. Schools, people group associations, and online stages can act as useful assets for dispersing data and moving activity.

Public commitment drives, including narratives, outreach projects, and resident science projects, add to building a worldwide local area of backers for manta beam protection. By imparting a feeling of obligation and worship for these marine marvels, instructive endeavors make ready for a future where manta beams flourish in sound seas.

5.2 Conservation Efforts and Success Stories

In the midst of the horde challenges looked by manta beams, an encouraging sign arises through devoted protection endeavors and moving examples of overcoming adversity. As these magnificent maritime animals explore the dangers presented by human exercises, a worldwide local area of researchers, traditionalists, policymakers, and nearby networks rallies to safeguard and protect manta beams and their environments. This investigation dives into the proactive measures attempted to protect manta beams, featuring examples of overcoming adversity that exhibit the positive effect of preservation drives.

1. **Laying out Marine Safeguarded Regions (MPAs): Places of refuge for Manta Beams**

   The foundation of Marine Safeguarded Regions (MPAs) remains as a foundation in the preservation of manta beams. These assigned zones limit human exercises, giving asylums where manta beams can take care of, mate, and conceive an offspring without the prompt dangers presented by fishing, territory corruption, and contamination.

   Nations, for example, Indonesia, a worldwide focal point for manta beam variety, have taken huge steps in MPA execution. Raja Ampat, a marine biodiversity area of interest inside Indonesian waters, brags one the world's most memorable manta beam safe-havens. The production of such zones shields basic territories as well as cultivates ecotourism, creating financial advantages for nearby networks while guaranteeing the drawn out practicality of manta beam populaces.

2. **Global Coordinated effort and Preservation Arrangements: Spanning Lines for Manta Beams**

Perceiving the transient idea of manta beams, worldwide coordinated effort and preservation arrangements assume a vital part in their security. The Show on Transient Species (CMS), a global arrangement under the Assembled Countries Climate Program, works with collaboration between countries to monitor transitory species.

Examples of overcoming adversity exude from cooperative endeavors, with nations like Ecuador driving the way. Ecuador, home to the world's biggest populace of goliath manta beams, executed a cross country restriction on the fishing and commodity of all manta beam items. Such unequivocal activities exhibit the force of global participation in relieving dangers and laying out a system for the supportable administration of manta beam populaces.

3. **Local area Based Protection: Engaging Watchmen of the Oceans**

Local area based preservation drives enable nearby networks to become watchmen of the oceans, effectively partaking in the assurance of manta beams and their environments. In locales where manta beams hold social importance, these drives influence conventional information and practices to make an amicable concurrence among people and marine life.

Fiji epitomizes the progress of local area based preservation. The foundation of privately overseen marine regions (LMMA) draws in networks in the maintainable administration of their marine assets. By ingraining a feeling of stewardship, these drives add to the protection of manta beam environments, guaranteeing the progression of their essential natural jobs.

4. **Logical Exploration and Ecotourism: Encouraging Comprehension and Appreciation**

Logical examination assumes a crucial part in disentangling the secrets of manta beams and illuminating protection systems. Progressing studies add to a more profound comprehension of their way of behaving, relocation designs, and environmental jobs, giving fundamental information to prove based preservation measures.

Ecotourism, when overseen capably, fills in as an incredible asset for preservation. The monetary advantages got from manageable natural life the travel industry can boost neighborhood networks to effectively safeguard manta beams and their territories. Objections like the Maldives grandstand how all around oversaw ecotourism can add to both protection and local area occupations.

5. **Regulation and Legitimate Assurances: Defending Manta Beams from Double-dealing**

Legitimate securities are instrumental in defending manta beams from abuse.

Nations all over the planet have perceived the direness of authorizing regulation to direct and confine exercises that compromise manta beam populaces. These lawful measures range from fishing boycotts to guidelines administering the exchange of manta beam items.

New Zealand remains as a signal of regulative activity, carrying out exhaustive security for manta beams. The species is presently completely safeguarded under the Untamed life Act, supporting the obligation to their protection and recognizing their natural worth to marine environments.

6. **Protection Schooling: Supporting a Worldwide People group of Backers**

Protection schooling fills in as an impetus for supporting a worldwide local area of backers focused on the prosperity of manta beams. Instructive drives, going from school projects to public mindfulness crusades, assume an essential part in dissipating legends, encouraging appreciation, and imparting a feeling of obligation towards marine preservation.

The Manta Trust, a non-benefit association committed to manta beam preservation, represents the effect of training. Their worldwide effort drives incorporate instructive materials, outreach projects, and resident science projects that draw in individuals, everything being equal, cultivating an aggregate comprehension of the significance of manta beam preservation.

7. **Recovery and Salvage Endeavors: Mending the Injuries of Human Effect**

In examples where manta beams succumb to human-actuated dangers, recovery and safeguard endeavors become essential. Associations and marine focuses furnished with the mastery to really focus on harmed or caught manta beams add to their recuperation and delivery back into nature.

Ocean World Orlando, for instance, has been associated with the salvage and restoration of manta beams. By resolving issues, for example, entrapment or injury, these endeavors offer another opportunity at life for individual manta beams and highlight the obligation to moderating the effect of human exercises.

8. **Mindful The travel industry Works on: Adjusting Preservation and Business**

The crossing point of the travel industry and preservation is a sensitive difficult exercise, and dependable the travel industry rehearses assume a critical part in this unique. Visit administrators, jump administrators, and untamed life lovers are progressively perceiving the significance of limiting aggravations to manta beams while giving open doors to dependable and instructive connections.

Bora in French Polynesia embodies the outcome of capable the travel industry rehearses. Nearby guidelines focus on the prosperity of manta beams by implementing rules that limit connections, guaranteeing a feasible harmony between the travel industry income and protection objectives.

9. **Examples of overcoming adversity from the Maldives: A Model for Manageable Practices**

The Maldives arises as a model for supportable manta beam the travel industry.

Through severe guidelines, the Maldivian government has made a structure that guarantees dependable connections with manta beams. Assigned cleaning stations and severe sets of rules have safeguarded the neighborhood manta beam populaces as well as added to the country's standing as a chief objective for moral marine the travel industry.

10. **Innovation and Resident Science: Outfitting Development for Preservation**

Progressions in innovation and the commitment of resident researchers add to an abundance of information essential for manta beam protection. Developments like satellite labeling, submerged robots, and photograph distinguishing proof data sets empower specialists and fans the same to contribute significant data about manta beam populaces, ways of behaving, and developments.

The web-based stage Manta Matcher, a worldwide data set for manta beam sightings and distinguishing pieces of proof, features the force of resident science.

Givers from around the world transfer pictures, adding to the aggregate information that illuminates protection methodologies and improves how we might interpret these cryptic marine animals.

5.3 Importance of Preserving Manta Ray Habitats for Pup Development

Safeguarding manta beam living spaces is principal for the fruitful improvement of manta beam puppies. These basic conditions, like waterfront regions and coral reefs, act as nurseries, giving sanctuary and bountiful food assets. The assurance of these environments guarantees the wellbeing of weak little guys during their beginning phases of life. By protecting these fundamental regions from dangers like contamination, living space debasement, and overfishing, we not just add to the prosperity of manta beam populaces yet additionally maintain the sensitive equilibrium of marine biological systems, encouraging the proceeded with development and strength of these wonderful maritime creatures.

Chapter 6

Technology And Research

In the huge spans of the world's seas, manta beams smoothly explore the profundities, dazzling the creative mind of researchers, moderates, and devotees the same. As these cryptic animals face developing dangers, innovation arises as an encouraging sign, offering inventive instruments that upset manta beam exploration and protection endeavors. This investigation digs into the crossing point of innovation and examination, unwinding the manners by which headways in logical techniques, GPS beacons, and resident science add to a more profound comprehension of manta beams and impel their preservation into what's in store.

1. **Satellite Labeling: Following the Sea Vagabonds**

   Satellite labeling remains as a distinct advantage in understanding the developments and ways of behaving of manta beams across tremendous maritime spreads. These super advanced gadgets, joined to the dorsal balances of manta beams, give constant information on their transitory examples, searching grounds, and maritime inclinations. The data gathered from satellite labeling contributes urgent bits of knowledge into the existence history of manta beams, unwinding secrets that were once concealed in the profundities.

   One of the spearheading drives in satellite labeling comes from specialists at Manta Trust, a non-benefit association committed to manta beam protection. Their venture, Manta Matcher, assembles information on individual manta beams as well as adds to a worldwide data set that illuminates protection techniques. Satellite labeling empowers scientists to recognize basic natural surroundings, relocation courses, and expected dangers, enabling traditionalists to configuration designated mediations for the security of manta beams.

2. **Acoustic Telemetry: Snoopping on Maritime Discussions**

   Acoustic telemetry arises as an integral asset for concentrating on the submerged developments and ways of behaving of manta beams. This innovation includes appending acoustic labels to manta beams, which transmit remarkable signs recognized by a variety of submerged collectors. The information gathered permits researchers to screen the developments of individual beams, uncovering their inclinations for explicit conditions and offering experiences into their social associations.

The utilization of acoustic telemetry in manta beam research is exemplified by tasks like the Worldwide FinPrint drive. By conveying acoustic collectors in manta beam environments, specialists gain a more profound comprehension of their spatial elements, assisting with recognizing key regions for security and survey the viability of preservation measures. Acoustic telemetry fills in as a quiet spectator, snoopping on the maritime discussions of manta beams and making an interpretation of them into significant data for protection endeavors.

3. **Visual ID Data sets: Countenances of the Profound**

Progressions in visual distinguishing proof data sets outfit the force of resident science to make exhaustive lists of individual manta beams. These information bases, frequently open on the web, permit analysts and devotees to contribute photos of manta beams, especially their remarkable ventral spot designs. Through design acknowledgment calculations, researchers can then recognize and follow individual beams over the long run.

MantaMatcher, started by the Marine Megafauna Establishment and presently incorporated with Manta Trust, represents the outcome of visual ID data sets. The stage empowers jumpers, picture takers, and specialists overall to transfer and match pictures, making a developing storehouse of manta beam characters. This cooperative methodology not just improves the comprehension of manta beam populaces yet additionally draws in people in general in the protection cycle, cultivating a worldwide local area of manta beam advocates.

4. **Submerged Robots and Remote Detecting: Eyes Underneath the Waves**

Submerged robots and remote detecting advances offer extraordinary admittance to the submerged domains where manta beams wander. These gadgets, furnished with high-goal cameras and sensors, give a non-nosy method for concentrating on manta beam natural surroundings, ways of behaving, and populace elements. From planning coral reefs to observing manta beam collections, submerged drones broaden the span of analysts underneath the waves.

The use of submerged drones in manta beam research is displayed in projects like the

XL Catlin Seaview Review. By catching all encompassing pictures of coral reefs and manta beam living spaces, specialists gain a comprehensive perspective on their surroundings. Remote detecting innovations, including satellite symbolism and flying studies, supplement submerged drone information, making a multi-faceted comprehension of the natural elements impacting manta beam populaces.

5. **Hereditary Examination: Opening the Code of Manta Beams**

Progressions in hereditary examination add to disentangling the hereditary code of manta beams, giving experiences into their populace design, availability, and transformative history. By dissecting DNA tests, analysts can evaluate hereditary variety, connection connections, and the effect of human exercises on manta beam populaces. This sub-atomic methodology improves preservation procedures by distinguishing unmistakable populaces and illuminating endeavors to safeguard their novel hereditary legacy.

Hereditary exploration on manta beams, exemplified by studies led by organizations like the Save Our Oceans Establishment, reveals insight into the network between various populaces. Understanding the hereditary construction of manta beam populaces is essential for planning protection estimates that think about the unmistakable requirements of explicit gatherings and locales. Hereditary examination turns into a critical device in the tool compartment of manta beam protection, offering a sub-atomic viewpoint on their complicated and interconnected lives.

6. **Computer generated Reality and Training: Jumping into Manta Beam Domains**

Computer generated reality (VR) advances rethink the limits of training and public commitment to manta beam preservation. VR encounters permit people to drench themselves in the submerged domains occupied by manta beams, encouraging a feeling of association and sympathy. These intelligent instructive devices assume a fundamental part in bringing issues to light, motivating activity, and supporting a worldwide local area of promoters for manta beam protection.

Projects like The Manta Beam Backers, which use VR to move clients into the universe of manta beams, embody the capability of this innovation. By giving a firsthand encounter of swimming close by these delicate monsters, VR teaches as well as fuels an enthusiasm for marine preservation. Computer generated reality turns into a scaffold between logical exploration and public commitment, welcoming people to become stewards of the seas from the solace of their homes.

7. **Man-made consciousness and AI: Deciphering Manta Beam Ways of behaving**

Man-made consciousness (computer based intelligence) and AI calculations are changing the examination of manta beam ways of behaving caught in immense datasets. These innovations cycle tremendous measures of submerged film, recognizing examples, ways of behaving, and drifts that might get away from the natural eye. From evaluating taking care of propensities to perceiving social collaborations, artificial intelligence and AI improve the proficiency and exactness of conduct studies.

Drives like Venture Manta computer based intelligence, a cooperation among scientists and innovation specialists, exhibit the use of AI in manta beam research.

Via preparing calculations to perceive explicit ways of behaving and includes, specialists can mechanize the examination of submerged film, saving time and assets. Computer based intelligence turns into a significant partner in the journey to unravel the complexities of manta beam ways of behaving, adding to a more nuanced comprehension of their natural jobs.

8. **Resident Science and Publicly supported Information: Saddling Worldwide Coordinated effort**

Resident science arises as a main thrust in manta beam research, tackling the aggregate force of fans, jumpers, and sea sweethearts all over the planet. Resident researchers contribute important information, going from manta beam sightings to social perceptions, essentially extending the extent of exploration drives. The democratization of logical information assortment connects with people in the preservation cycle and changes them into dynamic members in the mission to safeguard manta beams.

Stages like MantaMatcher and Manta Trust's web based announcing devices epitomize the progress of resident science in manta beam research. By welcoming general society to share their perceptions, scientists access an abundance of data that would be generally difficult to get. Resident science upgrades the amount of information as well as encourages a feeling of worldwide local area, joining individuals from different foundations in the common objective of manta beam protection.

9. **Ecological DNA (eDNA): Hints of Manta Beams in the Water**

Ecological DNA (eDNA) examination presents a painless way to deal with concentrating on manta beams by recognizing hints of their hereditary material in water tests. As manta beams travel through their territories, they shed skin cells, scales, and organic liquids, abandoning a hereditary unique mark. By examining eDNA, scientists can survey the presence and overflow of manta beams in unambiguous regions, offering a practical and negligibly meddling strategy for observing populaces.

Studies utilizing eDNA, for example, those led by the College of Salford's Manta Watch program, exhibit the capability of this innovation. By gathering water tests from manta beam living spaces, specialists can acquire experiences into their dissemination and overflow without direct connection. eDNA examination supplements conventional exploration strategies, giving an exhaustive comprehension of the biological elements of manta beam conditions.

6.1 Technological Advances in Studying Manta Ray Pup Development

Manta beams, the magnificent goliaths of the sea, have long enthralled the interest of researchers and protectionists. Among the most slippery parts of their lives is the improvement of manta beam puppies — the early sections of their life cycle that unfurl in the tremendous and frequently distant maritime domains. Mechanical advancements have arisen as significant instruments, revealing insight into the secrets of manta beam little guy improvement. This investigation dives into the bleeding edge of logical progressions, unwinding the job of innovation in concentrating on the sensitive and tricky beginning phases of manta beams.

1. **Satellite Labeling of Pregnant Females: Following the Excursion of Hopeful Moms**

   Satellite labeling has altered how we might interpret manta beam regenerative science, especially the developments of pregnant females as they explore the maritime spreads to conceive an offspring. Appending satellite labels to pregnant manta beams permits researchers to follow their transitory examples, giving bits of knowledge into the areas of basic environments for growth and pupping.

   In the Maldives, an eminent manta beam area of interest, specialists from the Manta Trust left on a historic undertaking to satellite label pregnant females. The information gathered uncovered the broad movements attempted by these eager moms, featuring the significance of explicit regions for pupping. By locating this data with natural boundaries, researchers gain a comprehensive perspective on the circumstances liked by pregnant manta beams, working with the distinguishing proof and security of urgent pupping grounds.

2. **Submerged Robots and Remote Checking: Looking into Manta Beam Nurseries**

   Submerged drones furnished with high-goal cameras and sensors give a non-meddlesome method for observing manta beam nurseries, where little guys spend their initial days. These mechanical wonders offer a brief look into the frequently hidden universe of manta beam pupping grounds, catching pictures and film that add to how we might interpret little guy conduct and communications with their current circumstance.

   In the waters off Mozambique, specialists used submerged robots to investigate potential manta beam pupping environments. The recording acquired permitted researchers to distinguish key elements of these areas, for example, shielded spaces and plentiful food sources. Remote observing of manta beam nurseries utilizing submerged drones upgrades preservation endeavors by giving basic data to the foundation of marine safeguarded regions (MPAs) devoted to defending these weak phases of manta beam life.

3. **Visual Distinguishing proof and Facial Acknowledgment: Recording the Novel Essences of Little guys**

   Similarly likewise with grown-up manta beams, visual distinguishing proof and facial acknowledgment innovations assume a urgent part in concentrating on manta beam little guys. The unmistakable spot designs on their ventral surfaces act as interesting identifiers, permitting scientists to follow individual puppies after some time. This harmless technique adds as far as anyone is concerned of little guy development rates, natural surroundings use, and populace elements. Projects like MantaMatcher, which have been instrumental in classifying and recognizing grown-up manta beams, stretch out their extension to incorporate little guys. By making extensive data sets of little guy personalities, analysts gain bits of knowledge into their developments, dispersal examples, and possible associations between various nurseries. The use of facial acknowledgment innovation guarantees a careful and exact examination of manta beam little guy improvement, cultivating a more profound comprehension of their initial life stages.

4. **Acoustic Telemetry on Puppies: Listening in on Adolescent Discussions**
   Acoustic telemetry, an innovation frequently applied to grown-up manta beams, is progressively being used to concentrate on the developments and ways of behaving of manta beam little guys. By joining acoustic labels to adolescent people, researchers can follow their developments inside nurseries and survey how natural variables impact their way of behaving. This innovation fills in as a virtual snoop, catching the submerged discussions of adolescent manta beams as they explore their living spaces.

   In locales like Hawaii, where manta beam nurseries are proven and factual, scientists convey acoustic telemetry to screen little guy conduct. The information got considers a definite investigation of their spatial inclinations, communications with conspecifics, and reactions to natural changes. Acoustic telemetry turns into a significant device in unraveling the beginning phases of manta beam little guy improvement, giving a window into their secret lives underneath the waves.

5. **Hereditary Investigation of Little guy Tissues: Unwinding Family Ties and Populace Elements**
   Headways in hereditary examination reach out to the investigation of manta beam little guys, offering bits of knowledge into their hereditary variety, parentage, and populace elements. Specialists gather tissue tests painlessly, frequently through little skin biopsies, to separate hereditary material for examination. The subsequent information add to how we might interpret the relatedness between people, the construction of manta beam populaces, and the expected effects of human exercises on their hereditary wellbeing.

   Concentrates on led in locales with realized manta beam nurseries, for example, Indonesia and Ecuador, consolidate hereditary examination to evaluate the relatedness of puppies and their moms. By disentangling family ties, scientists can assess the degree of inbreeding, recognize unmistakable hereditary populaces, and illuminate preservation techniques that consider the special hereditary legacy of manta beam nurseries.

6. **Natural DNA (eDNA): Following Little guy Presence in the Waters**
   Natural DNA (eDNA) examination arises as a harmless procedure for identify-

ing the presence of manta beam little guys in their living spaces. As puppies shed skin cells, scales, and natural liquids, they abandon hints of their hereditary material in the water. Gathering water tests permits researchers to remove and dissect eDNA, giving a financially savvy and insignificantly nosy strategy for checking little guy populaces.

In the waters of realized manta beam nurseries, specialists send eDNA testing to affirm the presence of puppies. This innovation supplements customary study strategies, offering a more proficient and extensive way to deal with observing little guy overflow and circulation. eDNA investigation adds to the foundation of pattern information for little guy populaces, working with long haul checking and preservation arranging.

7. **Resident Science and Local area Contribution: Eyes on Little guy Sightings**
Resident science assumes an imperative part in concentrating on manta beam little guy improvement by connecting with networks and fans in information assortment endeavors. People furnished with cameras and cell phones become dynamic members in reporting little guy sightings, contributing important data to continuous examination drives. This cooperative methodology not just grows the geographic extent of little guy observing yet additionally cultivates a feeling of stewardship among nearby networks.

Projects like MantaMatcher, which include resident researchers in recording manta beam people, stretch out their scope to incorporate little guy sightings. By empowering general society to report and share data on little guy experiences, specialists access an abundance of information that improves how we might interpret puppy dispersion, conduct, and environment use. Resident science turns into a scaffold between logical request and local area contribution, making a common obligation regarding the protection of manta beam little guys.

8. **Augmented Reality (VR) and Instructive Effort: Carrying Little guy Advancement to the Majority**

Computer generated Reality (VR) innovations offer an extraordinary way to deal with teaching general society about manta beam little guy improvement. VR encounters permit people to drench themselves in the realm of manta beam nurseries, seeing the beginning phases of little guy life in a virtual climate.

This imaginative instructive device fills in as a strong method for bringing issues to light, cultivating compassion, and motivating activity for the preservation of these weak marine creatures.

Projects like The Manta Beam Supporters use VR to carry manta beam little guy improvement to crowds all over the planet. By giving a firsthand encounter of little guy environments, ways of behaving, and connections, VR rises above geological limits and changes instructive effort. VR turns into a course for interfacing individuals with the secret sections of manta beam little guy improvement, developing a worldwide local area of promoters for their insurance.

6.2 Tracking and Monitoring Manta Ray Pups

The beginning phases of a manta beam's life stay hidden in secret underneath the tremendous scope of the sea. To unwind the mysteries of manta beam little guy improvement, researchers utilize a set-up of state of the art innovations that empower following and observing. This innovative odyssey into stowed away domains permits analysts to follow the excursions of these lofty maritime creatures from birth, revealing insight into their ways of behaving, living spaces, and weaknesses.

1. **Satellite Labeling: Following the Maritime Wanderings of Little guy Life**

   Satellite labeling arises as a progressive device for following manta beam puppies, empowering scientists to follow their maritime wanderings. By connecting satellite labels to the dorsal blades of puppies, researchers gain constant information on their developments, giving essential bits of knowledge into transitory examples, natural surroundings use, and potential dangers looked during early life stages.

   The satellite labeling of manta beam puppies contributes not exclusively to individual following yet additionally to the recognizable proof of basic natural surroundings. Following information uncovers the tremendous distances covered by little guys, revealing insight into their associations with sea flows and explicit natural circumstances. This innovation improves how we might interpret little guy conduct as well as educates the foundation regarding marine safeguarded regions (MPAs) committed to shielding these weak phases of manta beam life.

2. **Acoustic Telemetry: Snoopping on Adolescent Discussions**

   Acoustic telemetry, at first applied to grown-up manta beams, has tracked down its direction into the investigation of adolescent people. By connecting acoustic labels to manta beam little guys, researchers can listen in on their submerged discussions, acquiring experiences into their ways of behaving, cooperations, and reactions to natural signs.

   In nurseries and pupping grounds, acoustic telemetry turns into an important device for observing the developments of adolescent manta beams. The information gathered assist specialists with grasping the spatial inclinations of little guys, offering a window into their regular routines. Acoustic telemetry gives a non-meddling method for following manta beam puppies in their regular environments, adding to the more extensive comprehension of their formative biology.

3. **Visual Recognizable proof and Facial Acknowledgment: Recording Individual Little guy Personalities**

   The utilization of visual recognizable proof and facial acknowledgment innovations stretches out to the domain of manta beam puppies. Extraordinary spot designs on the ventral surfaces of people act as particular identifiers, permitting scientists to record and track individual little guy personalities over the long run. Projects like MantaMatcher, which have been instrumental in listing grown-up manta beams, presently integrate little guy distinguishing proof into their data sets. The fastidious documentation of individual puppies empowers researchers to concentrate on development rates, dispersal examples, and populace elements. The incorporation of facial acknowledgment innovation upgrades the exactness of information examination, adding to a more profound comprehension of manta beam little guy improvement.

4. **Submerged Robots and Remote Detecting: Looking into Nurseries with Accuracy**

Submerged drones furnished with high-goal cameras and sensors offer an exact method for looking into manta beam nurseries. These mechanical wonders furnish specialists with remarkable admittance to pupping grounds, catching pictures and film that add to the investigation of little guy conduct and communications with their current circumstance.

In locales where manta beam nurseries are known, submerged drones become fundamental devices for remote observing. The recording got offers important experiences into the highlights of these natural surroundings, including shielded spaces and plentiful food sources. Remote detecting innovations, including satellite symbolism and ethereal reviews, supplement submerged drone information, making a complex comprehension of the natural elements impacting manta beam little guy improvement.

5. **Hereditary Investigation of Little guy Tissues: Unwinding Genealogies and Availability**

Headways in hereditary examination reach out to the investigation of manta beam puppies, unwinding the intricacies of their ancestries and availability. Scientists gather tissue tests harmlessly, frequently through little skin biopsies, to remove hereditary material for examination.

The subsequent information add to how we might interpret relatedness between people, the construction of little guy populaces, and the effect of human exercises on their hereditary wellbeing.

Concentrates on led in districts with realized manta beam nurseries consolidate hereditary examination to survey the relatedness of puppies and their moms. By disentangling family ties, analysts can assess the degree of inbreeding, distinguish particular hereditary populaces, and illuminate preservation methodologies that consider the special hereditary legacy of manta beam nurseries.

6. **Ecological DNA (eDNA): Following Little guy Presence in the Waters**

Ecological DNA (eDNA) examination arises as a harmless procedure for identifying the presence of manta beam puppies in their living spaces. As little guys shed skin cells, scales, and natural liquids, they abandon hints of their hereditary material in the water. Gathering water tests permits researchers to remove and break down eDNA, giving a savvy and negligibly meddlesome strategy for observing little guy populaces.

In the waters of realized manta beam nurseries, specialists convey eDNA examining to affirm the presence of little guys. This innovation supplements conventional review techniques, offering a more productive and complete way to deal with observing little guy overflow and circulation. eDNA examination adds to the foundation of gauge information for little guy populaces, working with long haul checking and protection arranging.

7. **Resident Science and Local area Inclusion: An Organization of Little guy Watchers**

Resident science turns into a powerful power in following and observing manta beam puppies by drawing in networks and lovers in information assortment endeavors. People furnished with cameras and cell phones become dynamic members in archiving little guy sightings, contributing important data to continuous exploration drives. This cooperative methodology not just grows the geographic extent of little guy checking yet in addition cultivates a feeling of stewardship among neighborhood networks.

Projects like MantaMatcher, which include resident researchers in classifying manta beam people, stretch out their range to incorporate little guy sightings. By empowering people in general to report and share data on little guy experiences, specialists access an abundance of information that upgrades how we might interpret puppy conveyance, conduct, and environment use. Resident science turns into an organization of little guy watchers, making a common obligation regarding the preservation of manta beam puppies.

8. **Augmented Reality (VR) and Instructive Effort: Crossing over Holes in Getting it**

Computer generated Reality (VR) innovations offer a groundbreaking way to deal with instructing the general population about manta beam little guy following and observing. VR encounters permit people to submerge themselves in the realm of manta beam nurseries, seeing the beginning phases of little guy life in a virtual climate. This creative instructive device fills in as a strong method for bringing issues to light, encouraging sympathy, and moving activity for the protection of these weak marine creatures.

Projects like The Manta Beam Promoters use VR to bring manta beam little guy following and checking to crowds all over the planet. By giving a firsthand encounter of little guy natural surroundings, ways of behaving, and collaborations, VR rises above geological limits and changes instructive effort. VR turns into an extension between logical request and local area commitment, permitting individuals to observe the mechanical accomplishments utilized in following and checking manta beam little guys.

6.3 Collaborative Initiatives and Research

In the immense fields of the world's seas, cooperative drives and exploration assume a vital part in disentangling the secrets of manta beams and guaranteeing their preservation. Manta beams, with their confounding ways of behaving and weakness to different dangers, require an aggregate exertion that traverses boundaries, disciplines, and networks. This investigation dives into the cooperative drives and examination attempts that unite researchers, protectionists, networks, and fans to shield the eventual fate of these glorious maritime creatures.

1. **Worldwide Coordinated efforts: Connecting Seas for Manta Preservation**

    Manta beams are worldwide residents, navigating huge maritime distances that rise above public limits. Worldwide joint efforts structure the foundation of manta beam examination and preservation, joining researchers and associations from various nations in a common obligation to understanding and safeguarding these marine goliaths.

    Drives like the Worldwide Manta Beam Program, a joint effort between Manta Trust and the Save Our Oceans Establishment, embody the force of global organizations. By pooling assets, aptitude, and information, specialists can direct far reaching concentrates on manta beam populaces, movements, and ways of behaving. These joint efforts work with the foundation of worldwide preservation methodologies that address the assorted difficulties looked by manta beams in their transient processes.

2. **Non-benefit Associations: Bosses of Manta Beam Protection**

    Non-benefit associations devoted to marine preservation arise as champions in the aggregate work to safeguard manta beams. These associations, driven by an enthusiasm for maritime wellbeing, lead research, carry out protection projects, and participate in promotion to address the complex difficulties looked by manta beams.

    Manta Trust, a noticeable non-benefit association, remains at the front of manta beam preservation. Through cooperative exploration projects, instructive drives, and local area commitment, Manta Trust adds to a more profound comprehension of manta beams and advances preservation measures. Non-benefit associations act as impetuses for change, directing the aggregate energy of the worldwide local area toward the safeguarding of manta beams and their territories.

3. **Resident Science: A Worldwide Organization of Manta Beam Backers**

    Resident science changes people into dynamic members in manta beam exploration and preservation. Devotees, jumpers, and sea sweethearts all over the planet become vital donors, giving significant information on manta beam sightings, ways of behaving, and environment use. This democratization of logical information assortment grows the extent of examination drives and encourages a feeling of worldwide local area.

Stages like MantaMatcher embody the outcome of resident science in manta beam research. By empowering the general population to share photos and perceptions of manta beams, scientists access an abundance of data that would be trying to get through customary strategies. Resident science improves the amount of information as well as imparts a feeling of obligation and association among people, making a worldwide organization of manta beam advocates.

4. **Scholarly Exploration: Progressing Logical Comprehension**

Scholarly foundations and specialists contribute fundamentally to the logical comprehension of manta beams. Through thorough investigations, information examination, and hands on work, scholarly exploration gives fundamental bits of knowledge into the science, environment, and conduct of these marine monsters. The joint effort among the scholarly world and different partners reinforces the underpinning of information required for viable preservation systems.

Research projects drove by sea life scholars and biologists add to the group of logical writing on manta beams. By investigating themes like conceptive science, transitory examples, and natural jobs, scholastic exploration reveals insight into basic parts of manta beam life. Joint efforts among the scholarly community and non-benefit associations intensify the effect of exploration discoveries, making an interpretation of them into noteworthy measures for preservation.

5. **Local area based Preservation: Engaging Nearby Stewardship**

The association of nearby networks is vital to the progress of manta beam preservation endeavors. Cooperative drives that engage networks to become stewards of their marine surroundings add to the reasonable concurrence of people and manta beams. By incorporating nearby information and viewpoints, these drives encourage a feeling of pride and obligation among local area individuals.

Local area based preservation projects, for example, those executed by Manta Confidence in a joint effort with waterfront networks, represent the positive effect of neighborhood commitment. By consolidating conventional information and including networks in examination and checking exercises, these drives add to the drawn out security of manta beam natural surroundings. Cooperative methodologies guarantee that protection endeavors are socially touchy and comprehensive, tending to the requirements of both human and marine networks.

6. **Industry Associations: Adjusting Preservation and Monetary Interests**

Coordinated efforts with ventures working in manta beam environments are fundamental for accomplishing a harmony among preservation and monetary interests. The travel industry, specifically, can fundamentally affect manta beam populaces, both decidedly and adversely. Cooperative drives that draw in with the travel industry plan to advance mindful practices that limit aggravations to manta beams and their territories.

Associations between preservation associations and the travel industry administrators, for example, those encouraged by Manta Trust's Mindful The travel industry program, embody the potential for positive coordinated effort. By laying out rules for moral natural life communications, teaching visit administrators, and advancing dependable the travel industry rehearses, these drives add to the economical pleasure in manta beams by guests while protecting the prosperity of the marine animals.

7. **Government and Strategy Commitment: Supporting for Legitimate Insurances**

Cooperative commitment with states and policymakers is pivotal for ordering legitimate insurances and preservation measures for manta beams. By cooperating with legislative bodies, preservation associations can advocate for the foundation of marine safeguarded regions, the guideline of fishing rehearses, and the execution of protection approaches that shield manta beam living spaces.

The foundation of lawful assurances for manta beams, remembering their consideration for the Show on Global Exchange Imperiled Types of Wild Fauna and Vegetation (Refers to) Informative supplement II, reflects fruitful coordinated efforts between preservation associations and states. These assignments add to the worldwide work to battle unlawful exchange, by controlling and checking the global exchange of manta beam items.

8. **Instructive Effort: Motivating the Up and coming Age of Preservationists**

Instructive effort drives act as cooperative undertakings to rouse the up and coming age of traditionalists and ecological stewards. By connecting with schools, instructive organizations, and general society, these drives bring issues to light about the significance of manta beams and the requirement for their protection. Cooperative endeavors in schooling foster a feeling of obligation and impart natural morals in people in the future.

Projects like The Manta Trust's instructive projects, which include coordinated efforts with schools and instructive establishments, represent the effect of instructive effort. By giving assets, educational plans, and connecting with materials, these drives enable teachers and understudies to find out about manta beams and their protection. Cooperative instructive endeavors make a far reaching influence, impacting perspectives and ways of behaving toward marine protection on a worldwide scale.

Chapter 7

Human-Manta Ray Interaction And Conservation

The crossing point among people and manta beams unfurls as a fragile dance, where experiences bring out stunningness and miracle, yet human exercises present possible dangers to these magnificent maritime creatures. Understanding the elements of human-manta beam association is fundamental for cultivating capable practices and creating protection systems that guarantee the prosperity and endurance of manta beam populaces. This investigation digs into the intricacies of human-manta beam association, the social meaning of these experiences, the difficulties presented by different human exercises, and the cooperative endeavors pointed toward saving these notorious marine animals.

1. **Social Importance and Fantasies: Manta Beams in Human Legend**
   Manta beams have long held social importance in different beach front networks, with their superb appearances frequently entwined with nearby fantasies and convictions. In certain societies, manta beams are respected as images of solidarity, shrewdness, and security. Alternately, in different practices, they might be related with strange notions or misguided judgments.
   Understanding the social setting of human-manta beam communications is pivotal for advancing positive commitment. Cooperative endeavors between preservation associations and nearby networks expect to connect social points of view, encouraging a common appreciation for these marine monsters. Training and effort drives make progress toward dispersing fantasies and advancing an amicable concurrence between manta beams and the networks that share their natural surroundings.

2. **Ecotourism: Adjusting Preservation and Monetary Interests**
   The ascent of manta beam ecotourism gives a novel open door to people to observe these delicate monsters in their regular living spaces. Dependable ecotourism rehearses mean to adjust the monetary advantages of the travel industry with the need to safeguard manta beams and their environments. Notwithstanding,

the expanded human presence in manta beam areas of interest additionally raises worries about expected influences on their way of behaving, wellbeing, and generally prosperity.

Cooperative drives between protection associations, visit administrators, and neighborhood networks try to lay out rules for mindful untamed life collaborations. This incorporates advancing non-meddling perception distances, limiting the utilization of blaze photography, and creating implicit sets of rules for visit administrators. By encouraging a harmonious connection among the travel industry and preservation, these endeavors mean to guarantee that manta beam ecotourism turns into a power for good in supporting their drawn out endurance.

3. **Dangers from Customary Works on: Exploring Social Practices**

   In certain districts, conventional practices and social convictions might present dangers to manta beams. For instance, the utilization of manta beam gill plates in customary medication or social functions can add to the decay of manta beam populaces. Tending to these dangers requires a sensitive harmony between regarding social legacy and protecting the eventual fate of these weak marine species.

   Coordinated efforts between preservation associations, neighborhood networks, and social pioneers center around finding elective practices that line up with protection objectives. Schooling and mindfulness programs assume a urgent part in featuring the environmental significance of manta beams and cultivating a feeling of obligation among networks to safeguard their marine legacy. By exploring these social subtleties with awareness, cooperative endeavors expect to move rehearses towards maintainable options that benefit the two people and manta beams.

4. **Fishing Tensions: Moderating Bycatch and Designated Fisheries**

   Fishing exercises, whether deliberate or inadvertent, present huge dangers to manta beam populaces. Bycatch in fisheries focusing on different species and designated fisheries for manta beams add to populace declines. Understanding the monetary inspirations driving these exercises is fundamental for creating viable preservation procedures.

   Cooperative drives including fisheries the board, preservation associations, and neighborhood networks try to moderate the effects of fishing pressures on manta beams. This incorporates the execution of bycatch decrease measures, for example, the utilization of circle snares and the presentation of rejection gadgets in fishing gear. Furthermore, designated endeavors mean to move towards reasonable fishing rehearses that focus on the soundness of marine environments and the protection of weak species like manta beams.

5. **Environmental Change: Tending to Worldwide Effects**

   Environmental change presents a worldwide test that influences marine biological systems, including those occupied by manta beams. Climbing ocean temperatures, sea fermentation, and changes in prey accessibility can have flowing consequences for manta beam populaces. Cooperative exploration tries between environment researchers, sea life scholars, and progressives expect to figure out these complicated connections and foster methodologies to moderate the effects of environmental change on manta beams.

Preservation drives additionally center around bringing issues to light about the job of manta beams in environment versatility. Sound populaces of manta beams add to the general equilibrium of marine environments, making them stronger to the effects of environmental change. By featuring these interconnected connections, cooperative endeavors look to rouse worldwide activity to address the main drivers of environmental change and safeguard the territories that manta beams rely upon.

6. **Preservation through Schooling: Moving Stewardship**

   Training arises as an integral asset in the preservation of manta beams, encouraging a comprehension of their environmental jobs and weaknesses. Cooperative instructive drives include schools, networks, and the more extensive public in finding out about the significance of manta beams and the effects of human exercises on their populaces.

   Associations between protection associations and instructive foundations work with the improvement of educational plans, outreach programs, and intelligent learning materials. These drives give logical information as well as rouse a feeling of stewardship and obligation regarding the prosperity of manta beams. By enabling people with data, cooperative training endeavors add to an aggregate obligation to protection.

7. **Resident Science: Drawing in the Worldwide People group**

   Resident science assumes a critical part in checking manta beam populaces and understanding human-manta beam communications on a worldwide scale. Cooperative stages and tasks support people, jumpers, and sea fans to contribute important information on manta beam sightings, ways of behaving, and dissemination.

   Drives like MantaMatcher epitomize the force of resident science in building a far reaching comprehension of manta beam populaces. By connecting with the worldwide local area in information assortment, scientists can get to data that would be trying to get through conventional means. Resident science changes people into dynamic members in the preservation cycle, making an organization of backers who add to the security of manta beams and their natural surroundings.

8. **Innovation and Exploration: Creative Answers for Preservation**

   The marriage of innovation and exploration offers creative answers for understanding and moderating the effects of human exercises on manta beams.

Cooperative ventures including researchers, specialists, and innovation specialists investigate the use of state of the art instruments like satellite labeling, acoustic telemetry, and submerged drones.

These innovative headways give continuous information on manta beam developments, conduct, and natural surroundings. For instance, satellite labeling permits analysts to follow transitory examples, while acoustic telemetry gives experiences into the spatial inclinations of manta beams. Coordinated efforts among innovation and exploration enable preservation endeavors with exact data, offering a proactive way to deal with relieving dangers and safeguarding manta beam populaces.

9. **Preservation Strategies and Support: Forming an Economical Future**

   Cooperative promotion endeavors are instrumental in forming preservation strategies that defend manta beams and their environments. Protection associations, analysts, and supporters cooperate to impact peaceful accords, public regulation, and nearby guidelines that influence the prosperity of these marine species.

   Consideration in peaceful accords, for example, the Show on Worldwide Exchange Imperiled Types of Wild Fauna and Greenery (Refers to), gives lawful securities to manta beams. Cooperative promotion tries to raise the situation with manta beams on local and public protection plans, encouraging a guarantee to feasible practices and the safeguarding of basic territories.

10. **Industry Joint effort: Dependable Practices for Manageability**

    Joint effort with ventures working in manta beam territories is fundamental for accomplishing a harmony among protection and financial interests. The travel industry administrators, fisheries, and different partners participate in cooperative endeavors to execute capable practices that limit aggravations to manta beams and their living spaces.

    Mindful the travel industry drives, for example, those advanced by Manta Trust's Capable The travel industry program, set rules for moral natural life communications. Cooperation with fisheries includes the turn of events and reception of maintainable fishing rehearses. These industry joint efforts intend to make an agreeable connection between human exercises and the prosperity of manta beam populaces.

11. **Supportable Improvement Objectives: Manta Beams as Ministers for Sea Wellbeing**

The preservation of manta beams lines up with more extensive worldwide objectives for reasonable turn of events and sea wellbeing. Cooperative endeavors that underline the interconnectedness of marine biological systems, biodiversity protection, and environment strength add to accomplishing Supportable Advancement Objectives (SDGs).

Manta beams act as envoys for SDG 14: Life Beneath Water, pushing for the protection and supportable utilization of marine assets. Coordinated efforts that address the dangers to manta beams likewise add to objectives connected with environment activity, biodiversity protection, and the prosperity of seaside networks. By outlining manta beam protection inside the setting of more extensive maintainability goals, cooperative drives gather backing and acknowledgment on a worldwide scale.

7.1 Responsible Tourism and Manta Ray Conservation

The convergence of capable the travel industry and manta beam protection frames a fragile dance between human pleasure and the prosperity of these great marine creatures. Manta beams, with their smooth developments and enthralling presence, have become central focuses for ecotourism exercises in different regions of the planet. As the ubiquity of manta beam the travel industry develops, so does the requirement for mindful practices that focus on the protection of these weak species and their natural surroundings. This investigation digs into the harmonious connection between capable the travel industry and manta beam preservation, looking at the effects of the travel industry on manta beams, the standards of dependable the travel industry, fruitful contextual investigations, and the cooperative endeavors forming an economical future.

1. **The Ascent of Manta Beam The travel industry: Adjusting Happiness and Protection**

   Manta beam the travel industry has encountered a flood in prominence as explorers look for exceptional and spectacular natural life experiences. Areas of interest like tropical reefs and taking care of grounds have become safe houses for vacationers anxious to observe the style of manta beams skimming through the water. While the travel industry gives financial advantages to neighborhood networks and brings issues to light about marine protection, it additionally brings potential difficulties that should be addressed to guarantee the drawn out prosperity of manta beam populaces.

2. **The Effect of The travel industry on Manta Beams: Exploring the Dangers**

   The deluge of vacationers to manta beam territories can present dangers to the prosperity of these marine species. Direct aggravations, for example, congestion, commotion, and actual contact, may upset normal ways of behaving and make pressure manta beams. Furthermore, the utilization of blaze photography and ill-advised plunging practices can unfavorably affect their delicate eyes and skin. Understanding the effects of the travel industry on manta beams is fundamental for executing successful protection systems. Cooperative examination endeavors between sea life researcher, protection associations, and the travel industry administrators intend to survey the stressors related with the travel industry and foster rules for mindful practices that limit adverse consequences on manta beams.

3. **Standards of Mindful The travel industry: A Structure for Concordance**

Capable the travel industry offers a system for adjusting the monetary advantages of the travel industry with the preservation needs of manta beams and their living spaces. A few key standards guide dependable the travel industry works on, encouraging an agreeable conjunction between human happiness and natural safeguarding:

Instruction and Mindfulness: Edifying Sightseers and Administrators

Mindful the travel industry puts major areas of strength for on instruction and mindfulness. Vacationers are furnished with data about the science, conduct, and protection status of manta beams before their experiences. Moreover, visit administrators go through preparing to guarantee they have an exhaustive comprehension of capable practices and can pass this information on to their visitors.

Sets of principles: Setting Rules for Dependable Communications

Creating and sticking to sets of principles is fundamental in dependable the travel industry. These rules frame the appropriate way of behaving and distance to be kept up with during manta beam experiences. They likewise deter exercises that could upset the regular ways of behaving of manta beams, for example, pursuing, contacting, or taking care of.

Supportable Works on: Limiting Natural Effect

Dependable the travel industry embraces manageability by limiting the natural effect of vacationer exercises. This incorporates utilizing eco-accommodating transportation, diminishing waste, and carrying out low-influence framework. Supportable practices plan to guarantee that travel industry doesn't debase the environments basic to the prosperity of manta beams.

Local area Contribution: Enabling Neighborhood Stewardship

Drawing in neighborhood networks in the travel industry drives is a center rule of liability. By including networks in dynamic cycles and guaranteeing they benefit monetarily from the travel industry, mindful practices add to the strengthening of nearby stewardship. This encourages a feeling of pride and obligation regarding the preservation of manta beams and their living spaces.

Preservation Financing: Supporting Manta Beam Assurance Endeavors

Dependable the travel industry frequently includes adding to protection endeavors through direct subsidizing. Visit administrators might dispense a piece of their returns to help neighborhood preservation projects, research drives, or local area based programs focused on manta beam security. This monetary help assumes a significant part in supporting protection exercises in manta beam areas of interest.

4. **Contextual analyses in Dependable Manta Beam The travel industry: Examples of overcoming adversity**

A few objections all over the planet have effectively executed dependable manta beam the travel industry works on, showing that maintainable conjunction among people and manta beams is feasible. Inspecting these contextual investigations gives bits of knowledge into the positive results of mindful the travel industry drives.

Hanifaru Straight, Maldives: A Model of Dependable Manta Beam The travel industry

Hanifaru Cove in the Maldives has earned global respect as a model for capable manta beam the travel industry. The cove fills in as a basic taking care of ground for manta beams, drawing in huge totals during the southwest rainstorm. To deal with the rising number of vacationers looking for manta beam experiences, the Maldives laid out a marine safeguarded region (MPA) around Hanifaru Inlet.

Severe guidelines, including restricted admittance for visit administrators and a preclusion on securing, have been executed to limit the effect of the travel industry on manta beams and their natural surroundings. Sightseers are expected to follow sets of rules that focus on the prosperity of the marine climate. The progress of Hanifaru Narrows as a capable manta beam the travel industry objective features the viability of proactive preservation measures.

Woman Elliot Island, Australia: People group Driven Protection

Woman Elliot Island on the Incomparable Hindrance Reef is prestigious for its energetic marine life, including manta beams. The island's travel industry tasks are driven by major areas of strength for a to dependable practices and local area inclusion.

The island's eco-resort participates in preservation drives, including natural surroundings rebuilding activities and exploration coordinated efforts with sea life scholars.

Sightseers visiting Woman Elliot Island are taught about the significance of limiting their natural effect. The island's administrators effectively add to manta beam exploration and preservation endeavors, exhibiting the potential for local area driven drives to make a maintainable harmony among the travel industry and protection.

Nusa Penida, Indonesia: Cooperative Protection

Nusa Penida, off the shore of Bali, Indonesia, is a focal point for manta beam the travel industry. Perceiving the monetary worth of manta beam experiences, nearby networks, preservation associations, and visit administrators have teamed up to carry out mindful the travel industry rehearses.

Sets of rules have been laid out to direct traveler conduct, and local area individuals effectively partake in checking and research endeavors. Income created from manta beam the travel industry adds to neighborhood economies and assets preservation programs. The progress of Nusa Penida features the positive results of cooperative endeavors in adjusting the travel industry and manta beam preservation.

5. **Cooperative Endeavors for Dependable Manta Beam The travel industry: Molding a Practical Future**

The excursion towards dependable manta beam the travel industry includes joint effort between different partners, including legislatures, neighborhood networks, visit administrators, and preservation associations. Key cooperative endeavors molding a practical future include:

Unofficial laws and Implementation: Strategy Backing for Capable Practices

States assume a pivotal part in molding the scene of manta beam the travel industry through guidelines and requirement components. Laying out marine safeguarded regions, upholding general sets of rules, and executing authorizing frameworks for visit administrators are fundamental stages in guaranteeing mindful practices.

Cooperative endeavors between government offices, preservation associations, and the travel industry can prompt the production of successful strategies that focus on manta beam protection. By integrating logical bits of knowledge into strategy choices, state run administrations add to the drawn out manageability of manta beam the travel industry.

Logical Exploration: Illuminating Capable Practices

Joint effort between sea life scholars and the travel industry works with progressing logical examination that illuminates mindful practices. Research projects zeroed in on manta beam conduct, populace elements, and natural surroundings usage contribute important experiences that guide the improvement of governing sets of rules and preservation procedures.

By cultivating associations among researchers and visit administrators, cooperative exploration guarantees that capable the travel industry rehearses depend on the most recent logical information. This iterative cycle takes into consideration versatile administration procedures that can develop with a more profound comprehension of manta beam nature.

Local area Commitment: Engaging Neighborhood Stewardship

Nearby people group living in closeness to manta beam territories are key partners in capable the travel industry drives. Cooperative endeavors include connecting with networks in dynamic cycles, giving monetary motivating forces to protection, and offering instructive projects that feature the biological significance of manta beams.

Local area based preservation drives engage neighborhood stewardship, making a deep satisfaction and obligation regarding the insurance of manta beams. Through organizations with nearby networks, dependable the travel industry turns into an instrument for reasonable improvement that lines up with both monetary and protection objectives.

Visit Administrator Partnerships: Setting Industry Principles

Partnerships and relationship of visit administrators devoted to dependable practices assume a urgent part in setting industry norms. By laying out rules, sharing accepted procedures, and advancing ceaseless schooling, these coalitions add to the professionalization of the manta beam the travel industry area.

Joint effort among visit administrators encourages a feeling of aggregate liability regarding manta beam preservation. Industry principles can assist with forestalling impractical works on, guaranteeing that administrators comply to moral rules that focus on the prosperity of manta beams and their living spaces.

Preservation Associations: Catalyzing Change

Non-benefit associations devoted to marine protection go about as impetuses for change in the dependable the travel industry scene. These associations take part in promotion, local area outreach, and cooperative tasks that line up with the objectives of manta beam assurance.

Cooperative endeavors between preservation associations, states, and the travel industry add to the advancement of protection programs, research drives, and instructive missions. By utilizing their mastery and organizations, these associations assume a fundamental part in catalyzing positive change inside the mindful the travel industry area.

6. **Difficulties and Amazing open doors: Exploring the Way ahead**

While dependable manta beam the travel industry has shown outcome in different areas, challenges persevere, and ceaseless endeavors are expected to explore the way ahead. Key difficulties and open doors include:

Requirement and Consistence: Spanning Holes in Execution

In spite of the foundation of guidelines and governing sets of rules, authorization and consistence remain difficulties in numerous objections. Fortifying cooperation between government specialists, protection associations, and neighborhood networks is fundamental to guarantee that capable the travel industry rehearses are actually implemented.

Potential open doors lie in creating imaginative checking and implementation systems, like the utilization of innovation and resident science. By crossing over holes in execution, cooperative endeavors can upgrade the adequacy of mindful the travel industry drives.

Traveler Training: Cultivating a Culture of Liability

The progress of mindful manta beam the travel industry relies on the training of vacationers. Overcoming any issues among mindfulness and dependable way of behaving requires continuous endeavors to encourage a culture of liability among guests. Cooperative drives including visit administrators, legislatures, and protection associations can upgrade instructive effort programs.

Amazing open doors exist to use advanced stages, intelligent shows, and vivid encounters to teach vacationers about the environmental meaning of manta beams.

By moving a feeling of stewardship, vacationer schooling turns into an amazing asset for significantly shaping capable way of behaving.

Environmental Change Versatility: Coordinating Protection into Environment Techniques

The effects of environmental change represent extra difficulties for manta beam preservation. Climbing ocean temperatures, sea fermentation, and changes in prey accessibility can influence the dispersion and conduct of manta beams. Cooperative endeavors ought to incorporate manta beam protection into more extensive environment flexibility procedures.

Amazing open doors exist to adjust capable the travel industry practices to environment cordial drives. Advancing manageable transportation, limiting carbon impressions, and supporting undertakings that address environmental change can add to the general strength of manta beam populaces.

Mechanical Advancements: Improving Checking and Exploration

The reconciliation of mechanical developments holds guarantee for improving observing and research in capable manta beam the travel industry. Cooperative activities that influence headways in satellite following, acoustic telemetry, and submerged robots can give continuous information on manta beam developments and conduct.

Open doors exist to draw in the travel industry in supporting and taking part in innovation driven research drives. By encouraging joint effort between researchers, innovation specialists, and visit administrators, inventive arrangements can add to a more profound comprehension of manta beam nature and illuminate dependable practices.

7.2 Educational Programs and Public Awareness

In the domain of manta beam protection, instructive projects and public mindfulness drives arise as incredible assets to rouse change and cultivate an aggregate obligation to defending these eminent marine animals. The outcome of preservation endeavors relies on the edification of people, networks, and people in the future about the biological significance of manta beams and the dangers they face. This investigation dives into the groundbreaking effect of instructive projects and public mindfulness crusades, explaining how these drives engage minds, support natural stewardship, and add to the more extensive objective of manta beam protection.

Instructive Projects: Enlightening the Marvels of Manta Beams

Instructive projects assume a critical part in enlightening the marvels of manta beams, unwinding the secrets of their science, conduct, and biological importance. These projects, frequently initiated by protection associations, sea life scientists, and instructive establishments, contact assorted crowds going from younger students to neighborhood networks and worldwide fans.

Through drawing in educational programs, intuitive studios, and vivid opportunities for growth, instructive projects give a window into the submerged domain of manta beams. They not just grandstand the magnificence of these maritime monsters yet in addition impart a profound appreciation for their imperative job in marine environments. By spreading logical information, scattering legends, and underlining the interconnectedness of marine life, instructive projects engage people with the comprehension expected to become advocates for manta beam preservation.

Public Mindfulness Missions: Catalyzing Change through Promotion

Public mindfulness crusades act as impetuses for change, utilizing the range of media, social stages, and local area commitment to disperse urgent data about manta beams and the protection challenges they face. These missions, frequently arranged by preservation associations and upheld by enthusiastic supporters, intend to raise manta beams into the public awareness and move activity.

Through convincing visuals, narratives, and narrating, public mindfulness crusades bring out sympathy and a feeling of obligation toward manta beams. They shed light on the dangers presented by environment debasement, environmental change, and human exercises, encouraging people to settle on informed decisions that add to the prosperity of these marine species. Public mindfulness turns into a main thrust for strategy backing, reasonable the travel industry rehearses, and the security of basic territories, cultivating a groundswell of help for manta beam preservation.

Enabling Personalities: The Way to Practical Conjunction

Instructive projects and public mindfulness drives combine in their central goal to engage minds, cultivating a feeling of ecological obligation and moral direct in the domain of manta beam preservation. By furnishing people with information about the delicacy of marine environments and the significance of biodiversity, these drives rouse a change in outlook in mentalities and ways of behaving.

Engaged personalities become representatives for manta beam protection, upholding for economical works on, supporting preservation projects, and affecting leaders. The gradually expanding influence of this strengthening reaches out past individual activities to incorporate local area wide change, making an organization of informed advocates who by and large endeavor to safeguard the seas and their occupants.

In the excursion toward reasonable concurrence with manta beams, the groundbreaking force of schooling and mindfulness radiates brilliantly. As psyches are illuminated, a tradition of stewardship is developed, guaranteeing that the seas, and the hypnotizing animals that possess them, flourish for a long time into the future. Through instructive illumination and public backing, the fragile dance among people and manta beams changes into an amicable ensemble of concurrence, where every individual assumes an essential part in protecting the miracles of the submerged world.

7.3 Balancing Tourism with Conservation

The fragile harmony among the travel industry and protection is a basic undertaking, especially in living spaces visited by great manta beams. These marine monsters draw in sightseers looking for spectacular experiences, giving monetary advantages to neighborhood networks while bringing issues to light about marine preservation. In any case, the flood in the travel industry presents difficulties to the prosperity of manta beams, requesting a cautious harmony to guarantee their protection.

Accomplishing concordance requires a diverse methodology. Capable the travel industry rehearses, directed by sets of rules and practical standards, assume a focal part. By restricting human effect through legitimate way of behaving, managed admittance, and adherence to moral rules, vacationers can coincide amicably with manta beams in their normal environments.

Coordinated effort between states, preservation associations, neighborhood networks, and the travel industry is crucial. Carrying out and implementing guidelines, making marine safeguarded regions, and taking part in local area based protection drives are fundamental stages. These endeavors look for not exclusively to relieve the adverse consequences of the travel industry yet in addition to use its true capacity as an impetus for marine preservation.

Offsetting the travel industry with preservation is a unique dance that requires continuous responsibility, flexibility, and a common vision of protecting the marvels of the submerged world. Through this sensitive harmony, humankind has the valuable chance to delight in the excellence of manta beams while shielding their living spaces for people in the future.